SHOULD WE USE
SOMEONE
ELSE'S
SERMON?

SHOULD WE USE SOMEONE ELSE'S SERMON?

Preaching IN A Cut-AND-Paste World

SCOTT M. GIBSON

ZONDERVAN®

ZONDERVAN.com/
AUTHORTRACKER
follow your favorite authors

ZONDERVAN

Should We Use Someone Else's Sermon?
Copyright © 2008 by Scott M. Gibson

This title is also available as a Zondervan ebook.
Visit www.zondervan.com/ebooks.

This title is also available in a Zondervan audio edition.
Visit www.zondervan.fm.

Requests for information should be addressed to:
Zondervan, *Grand Rapids, Michigan* 49530

Library of Congress Cataloging-in-Publication Data

Gibson, Scott M., 1957 –
    Should we use someone else's sermon : preaching in a cut-and-paste world /
Scott M. Gibson.
       p. cm.
    Includes bibliographical references.
    ISBN 978-0-310-28673-8 (softcover : alk. paper)
    1. Preaching. 2. Plagiarism. I. Title.
BV4211.3.G53 2008
251 – dc22   2008016705

Interior design: Ben Fetterley

Printed in the United States of America

To Rhonda,
who stole my heart.

CONTENTS

ACKNOWLEDGMENTS

They came and prigged my silver,
my linen and my store,
But they couldn't prig my sermons;
they had all been prigged before.

—E. V. Lucas, from the novel **Mr. Ingleside**

I'm grateful to Wayne Shaw and Chuck Sackett for the kind invitation for me to deliver the Webb Lectures on Preaching at Lincoln Christian College and Seminary in the fall of 2005. This opportunity to speak to students, faculty, and alumni on the topic of preaching and plagiarism was the catalyst that enabled me to put onto paper my research and reflections. Thanks to Wayne and Chuck and those in attendance for your feedback and interaction.

The opportunity to lecture on preaching and plagiarism at Regent College, Vancouver, British Columbia, during the spring school of 2007, gave me further occasion to test my thinking. Thank you for this privilege.

Thanks to Jeffrey Arthurs, Haddon Robinson, Matthew Kim, Casey Barton, Patricia Batten, Calvin Choi, Eric Dokken, and Lee Eclov for your insights from reading various drafts of the project. Thanks, too, to Grant Buchholtz, Keith Campbell, Joy Carren, Aaron Chan, Holgie Choi, Michael Curtis, David Hanke, Thomas V. Haugen, Lisa Morrison, Bill Nicoson, Stephen Nyakairu, Gustin Oh, John Percival, Deryk Richenburg, Mike Samson, Stephen Sebastian, Ken Shigematsu, Brian Shockey, Ken Swetland, and Samuel Yu.

Many thanks to the Board of Trustees of Gordon-Conwell Theological Seminary for the generous gift of sabbatical study, during which I researched and wrote this book. Thank you, thank you, thank you.

I'm grateful to John V. Tornfelt, academic dean at Evangelical School of Theology in Meyerstown, Pennsylvania, for permission to use his case study and teaching notes for "Whose Sermon Is It?" John's interest in the subject of preaching and plagiarism helped as I honed the chapters of this book.

A thousand thanks to Paul Engle of Zondervan for your wisdom, insight, and support for this project. Years ago Paul gave me, a fledgling junior professor of preaching, an opportunity to publish, for which I continue to be grateful. Once again I have the pleasure of working with him. Your understanding and interest in the subject and your suggestions and encouragement have sustained this project more than you can imagine. Thanks also to Verlyn Verbrugge and intern Karin Walters at Zondervan for your expert and careful editing of this project. I appreciate it more than you know.

Tobias Wolff wrote *Old School*, a novel about a student who plagiarized a short story while studying at an exclusive boy's school. The boy pilfered a story that was written a few years earlier by a female student from the neighboring girl's school. At the time of the accusation, the president of the student honor council said despairingly to the plagiarist, "Plagiarism's bad enough.... But from a girl? I can't believe you'd plagiarize from a girl."[1] However, I know a girl who's worth stealing from, my wife, Rhonda. She has shown me what it means to love. She is patient, attentive, constant in her faith, and worth copying.

So, this book on sermon stealing is dedicated to my wife, Rhonda, who stole my heart. She kidnapped me and has held me ransom with love. Her support, care, and grace have changed my life. Hers is an appropriate theft—one for which I'll be ever thankful to the Lord, and by which I'm truly blessed.

CHAPTER

ONE

SCENES OF SERMON STEALING

If it happens that a preacher weaves among his own words a proportion of other men's flowers, he falls into worse disgrace than a common thief.

—John Chrysostom

SCENE ONE: FLAP IN FELLOWSHIP HALL

The first time I faced the ugliness of plagiarism was when I was sixteen years old. It was the days of the Jesus Movement, and as a new Christian I was involved in every Bible study or any other kind of study. One of the studies I participated in was a reading group consisting of men and women of all ages. We met weekly, reading through popular Christian books. We read a chapter or two for each week's meeting and discussed it.

While at worship one Sunday morning at my home church, the preacher talked in his sermon about an incident that happened to him that week. He described a scene that took place in the middle of the night as he tended to his little girls. The setting, the words, the mood—everything—came from the book our group was reading.

As the congregation filtered out of the building, one of the leaders of the group—Don, a middle-aged man—confronted the pastor while he was shaking hands at the door. "You used a story from Keith Miller, didn't you?" he queried. He challenged him a little more. The pastor was shaken. He mumbled and fumbled, but the accusations did not move any further—until later that afternoon.

I was home when the telephone rang. My mother called me to the phone.

"It's Mr. Cunningham," she said. I knew Mr. Cunningham. He was the head deacon, a retired farmer who had given his life to the church. Mr. Cunningham was always kind to me. He knew I didn't come from a Christian home and was happy that I had become part of the church.

"Hello," I said.

"Hello, Scott, this is Mitchell Cunningham." His voice seemed formal, business like. "The reason why I'm calling is that you're to come to a deacon's meeting next Sunday afternoon. We want to talk with you about the accusations your reading group has against the pastor." My heart sank. I began to tremble. I really didn't know what to think. But, as a young, naïve high school kid, I agreed to be at the meeting.

The next week, the entire reading group assembled in the Fellowship Hall, along with the deacons and deaconesses. A long series of tables stretched the length of the hall to fit us all around the table—to resemble fellowship, I guess. I knew something important and strangely odd was happening, but, to my young mind, I really didn't fully comprehend it.

Mr. Cunningham called the meeting to order and led in prayer. He began by stating that the meeting was called because our reading group had accused the pastor of plagiarizing.

"Your group is causing all kinds of problems in this church," piped one of the deaconesses.

"Leave the pastor alone!" shouted another.

"What is happening?" I thought. The meeting deteriorated into a cesspool of accusations. Tempers flared. But the issue of what the pastor actually did—or did not do—was never addressed. The problem became ours, not his. I knew then what was happening: we were on the edge of being kicked out of the church.

However the matter was handled or mishandled, I am pained every time I recall the incident. I am hurt that my reading group was so easily indicted. I am distressed that the pastor appeared to have gotten off so simply. I am concerned that the pastor seemed to use another's material as if it were his own and didn't even try to clear up the matter for us—and the deacon board. Mind you, I was not raised in a Christian home. I was a sixteen-year-old kid who knew very little about church and the Bible, but I did know that something was not right. Yet with the way I was treated as a new Christian, I could have walked away from church forever. I could have pitched the faith. But I didn't. I guess I knew that we're all sinners—me too—and we're all in need of grace. And God's grace had ahold of me.

At that meeting and in that church I observed the power of plagiarism. The confusion and potential catastrophe just one little misrepresentation makes has long-lasting consequences. Not until years later did I meet again the ugliness of plagiarism and observed once more the poison it produces in a church and in the soul.

SCENE TWO: CONFRONTATION ON A COLD NEW ENGLAND NIGHT

Plagiarism is stealing someone else's words or thoughts and claiming them as your own. The Latin root—*plagiarius*—means kidnapper. The thief called plagiarism has been around a long time. He hides in the computer keyboards of novelists. He creeps into student dorm rooms. He can be found on the front page of any newspaper. He ruins science projects and causes havoc in the classroom. He can be found tempting theologians, and he often trips up preachers.

You may even have encountered this thief yourself. Maybe you have colluded with him in some clandestine thievery, or you have been tempted to follow his lead down the path of least resistance. He is tricky and wily. And, as I told you, I have met him myself. He has a long history, and not everyone agrees on what he looks like.

I assure you, I have seen him. I have smelled him. I have seen his victims up close. And I have been tempted myself, and I live to tell it. At this point, I am all grown-up and my second encounter with plagiarism took place on a cold winter evening. Winter evenings in New England are particularly unpleasant. The night is dark, the air is wet, and all one feels is cold.

The telephone rang, and on the other end was the head deacon, Rob, who told me there was an important meeting at the church to which I was summoned. I had been a deacon at our church for the previous three years. I kissed my wife good-bye and told her that I was sure the meeting would not last long. I was wrong, for I came to discover that our pastor was a kidnapper. No, he was not in jail, but he was a prisoner of his own devices. He had plagiarized the entire series he was preaching. And he got caught. The evening got even colder.

The deacons sat around the pastor's study uncomfortably hearing the charges brought by the one who discovered the plagiarism. His words were gentle and firm, yet piercing. The pastor tearfully confessed his misdeed. We deacons were numb. It was not that we could not imagine that the pastor had plagiarized, but it was something we simply never expected. I felt like I did when I was at the deacons' meeting on that dismal Sunday afternoon. Something important and strangely odd was happening.

We knew we had to do something. We were the deacons. We just listened to an accusation, an admission, and a plea for forgiveness. First, we prayed. We really needed wisdom. We were walking into the black of night and weren't really sure where we were going. We had no map. We really didn't have a dependable flashlight either. Sure, the Bible says, "Do not steal," but does this apply to sermons? We didn't know.

"At least this is better than my earlier encounter with plagiarism," I thought. Then, the culprit was me — us, the reading group; now, at least the transgressor became a confessor. He admitted his wrongdoing. But, like the board of deacons on which I served, there are numerous questions we face: What are churches — boards, committees, and congregations — to do with preachers who plagiarize? What are preachers to do? How can preachers fend off the temptation to copy and preach someone else's sermon or illustrations as if they were his or her own? What can preachers who get caught up in the alluring attraction of plagiarism do to change, to resist its enticing ways? That is what this book is about.

These two instances, one from my youth and the other from more recent days, have combined to pique my interest in the history of, occurrence of, attitude toward, definition of, and ethics of plagiarism. They frame my thinking on this important spiritual, practical, and ethical matter. The intention of this small book is to get to the bottom of the practice of plagiarism, this sermon stealing, to consider the background of plagiarism, to explore a definition of it, and to determine some principles of a biblical ethic for putting together sermons in a cut-and-paste world.[1]

THINK ABOUT IT

1. Have you listened to a sermon you suspected was plagiarized? How did you respond?
2. Have you ever preached someone else's sermon or used an illustration that was not yours, but stated it as if it were? What motivated you to do it?
3. What are your concerns, if any, about plagiarism and preaching?
4. As you begin reading this book, what is your attitude toward preaching and what would you like to learn about it?

CHAPTER

TWO

THE LONG LEGACY OF SERMON STEALING

Plagiarize!
Let no one else's work evade your eyes.
Remember why the good Lord made your eyes.
So don't shade your eyes,
But plagiarize, plagiarize, plagiarize,
Only be sure always to call it, please—research.[1]

—Lobachevsky, A song by Tom Lehrer

ALL OVER THE PLACE

Did you know that the practice of plagiarism is not just a preacher's problem but its fingerprints are found all over the place? In fact, this interloper infects more than just preachers: she intrudes into numerous occupations wreaking havoc, destroying callings and careers. I've discovered that the history of plagiarism in preaching is long and that the attitudes toward plagiarism in preaching vary.

Prints Pop Up in the Literary World

Famous novelist Mark Twain was accused of plagiarism by a Mr. Goodman of Virginia City, a man with whom he had served on the town's newspaper. Goodman said that Twain plagiarized his dedication in *Innocents Abroad* from Oliver Wendall Holmes's dedication in Holmes's book of poems. It turns out that some years before *Innocents Abroad* was published (in 1869), Twain was on Hawaii's Big Island. He rode a horse all over the island and ended up getting a terrible case of saddle sores, taking two weeks to recover. During his lonely recovery, all he had to read was Holmes's book of poems. So, as he says, "They kept me in my room, unclothed and in persistent pain, for two weeks, with no company but cigars and the little volume of poems. Of course I read them almost constantly; I read them from beginning to end, then began in the middle and read them both ways. In a word, I read the book to rags and was infinitely grateful to the hand that wrote it."[2]

One doesn't need to look into the nineteenth century to get confirmed cases of literary plagiarism. Noted historians Stephen E. Ambrose and Doris Kearns Goodwin were accused of blatant plagiarizing.[3] Added to this list is Christopher Sawyer-Laucanno, an E. E. Cummings scholar, who was accused of "wholesale borrowing" from Richard S. Kennedy's 1980 biography on Cummings. Sawyer-Laucanno acknowledged that "he failed to credit some passages that were based substantially on Kennedy's book," and that he was "dismayed by what he termed an oversight in documenting his sources" and that "the mistakes were unintentional."[4]

The Harvard coed Kaavya Viswanathan admitted she plagiarized portions of her hit debut novel, *How Opal Mehta Got Kissed, Got Wild, and Got a Life*.[5] The book was pulled from the shelves and was not reissued.[6]

Plagiarism in the Entertainment Industry

In the entertainment industry we can see plagiarism taking a gloating bow. Jay Leno accused Judy Brown, a comedy teacher and joke book writer, of stealing his jokes.[7] Art Buchwald and Alain Bernheim sued Paramount Pictures claiming that Eddie Murphy stole from Buchwald's column the idea for the movie *Coming to America*. Buchwald and Bernheim proved in court that Buchwald had come up with the original idea and was not given credit nor was he compensated.[8]

Plagiarism Shows Up at School

The Rutgers' Management Education Center took a national survey of 4,500 high school students and found that 75 percent of them engaged in serious cheating, with more than half having plagiarized work they found on the Internet.[9] In a similar survey, *Education Week* found that 54 percent of students they polled admitted to plagiarizing from the Internet. The survey also found that 74 percent admitted that they had committed "serious" cheating at least once during the past school year.[10]

About thirty years ago, Hunter Beckelhymer lamented in an article about a seminary student (Student A) who submitted a sermon outline. Beckelhymer recognized it as a sermon outline by a nationally known preacher (Preacher B) on the East Coast. The story he tells goes like this: Beckelhymer talked to the student, who admitted to the plagiarism. However, the student said that he had actually taken it not from the preacher from the East Coast, but from another preacher (Preacher C).

Beckelhymer told a faculty member (Professor D) about the incident, and the professor stated that this was a case of poetic justice. Beckelhymer explained what the professor meant: On an eastern trip not long since, the professor had gone to morning worship in the church of Preacher B, whom he greatly admired. It chanced that on that particular Sunday, Preacher B used almost verbatim a sermon by Preacher E, which sermon Professor D had included with due credit in an anthology of sermons he had edited. When he met Professor D at the door afterwards, Preacher B's embarrassment was acute. He had been caught in an impossible time-bind that week, he said, and had resorted under pressure to a practice he deplored, had rarely if ever indulged in before, and would certainly never follow again — sentiments very like those expressed to me by Student A.

Beckelhymer concludes, "This is surely a remarkable case of homiletical hanky-panky."[11] College students and seminary students are tempted by plagiarism and some even engage in it — then and now.

Plagiarism Plagues the Field of Journalism

Accused plagiarist and reporter Jack Kelley of *USA Today* and his managing editor, Hal Ritter, lost their jobs over a plagiarism flap.[12] The *Columbia Journalism Review* conducted a study of twenty newspapers and magazines where plagiarism cases took place between 1988 and 1995. Trudy Lieberman reports:

> Eight reporters were fired. Two of them were rehired after Newspaper Guild arbitrations, and the rest have secured new positions, some in journalism. Three of the twenty were suspended for varying lengths of time; one had his column suspended for a brief period; one had his column discontinued but kept his job; one resigned and was offered another job at the same organization; one left the paper before his plagiarism was discovered, and the remaining five were not punished. [13]

A Worcester, Massachusetts newspaper fired its New England Patriots reporter for plagiarism. He allegedly stole material from *Sports Illustrated* writer Peter King.[14] *New York Times* reporter Jayson Blair fabricated and plagiarized numerous stories and was fired.[15]

Plagiarism Is Found on the Professor and in the Military

William W. Meissner, a professor at Boston College, "committed a 'serious breach of professional and scholarly standards' by recycling another professor's ideas in a recent book on psychoanalysis without acknowledging their source, according to the Boston Psychoanalytic Society, which investigated the book's scholarship last year." Meissner's book, *The Ethical Dimension of Psychoanalysis: A Dialogue*, published in 2003, closely echoes the phrasing and ideas in *Psychoanalysis and Ethics* by Ernest Wallwork, published in 1991.[16]

On a similar note, *New York Times* writer Edward Rothstein reported another case:

> John L. Casti, a science writer who teaches at the Technical University of Vienna and at the Santa Fe Institute in New Mexico, has been accused of lifting a substantial number of extended passages from other sources in his latest book, "Mathematical Mountaintops: The Five Most Famous Problems of All Time" (Oxford 2002). Mr. Casti's book, written for the lay reader, describes mathematicians' explorations of complicated ideas involving maps, numbers and spaces. But along the way Mr. Casti's research apparently got a bit out of hand. [17]

Widening the angle to general education, one finds the falsifying and plagiarizing installment of the Edward Waters College accreditation review in 2004. The "Quality Enhancement Plan" supposedly drawn up by the college was actually plagiarized from the "Quality Enhancement Plan of Alabama A&M University." The accreditation was rescinded and the president was led to resign.[18] Another president resigned for plagiarizing a speech at freshman orientation. Hamilton College president, Eugene M. Tobin, apologized that he "did not provide sufficient attribution to all its various sources" in his speech.[19]

Consider the squeaky-clean environs of the military promotion process. Soldiers who passed the exam were able to speed up promotions and pay increases.[20] Promotion exam information was traded on the Internet. Army Specialist Adam Chrysler, operator of ShamSchool.com, thought posting exams was a way for soldiers to help other soldiers.[21] Clearly this is a case of soldiers helping other soldiers — to cheat.

Theologians Do It Too

Even theologians have gotten tangled up in the web of plagiarism. In an early example, exponent of Natural Theology and author of a book by the same title, William Paley was cited with plagiarizing from Dutch theologian Bernard Nieuwentyt's work published in Amsterdam in 1700.[22] Nineteenth-century preacher Henry J. Fox commented on a similar case of plagiarism:

> In an exhaustive sketch of the "Life of Professor George Lawson," Professor Edward A. Park, of Andover, after acknowledging with most refreshing naivete that he had borrowed from Dr. Mac Farlane "a large part of his biographical essay," makes, on the authority of the author to whom he is so largely indebted, the following terrible charge: "A living (in 1842) and distinguished American commentator has, in his exposition of the Book of Genesis, made an unwarranted use of Dr. Lawson's 'Lecture on Joseph.' From the thirty-seventh chapter to the end of Genesis a large portion is plagiarized from the Scotch expositor — we should say to the extent of two thirds of the whole.[23]

Closer to our day is the case of Catholic columnist Richard McBrien who allegedly stole material from another author.[24] Others involved in Christian publication have had the nasty word "plagiarist" waged against them. Advancing the Ministries of the Gospel (AMG) settled with Moody Press for the use of unauthorized material from one of Moody's books on studying the Old Testament.[25]

Even religions labeled as questionable participate in plagiarism. It's claimed that the works of Joseph Smith, founder of the Mormons, and the writings of Ellen G. White of the Seventh Day Adventists are filled with writings from others. *Update: A Quarterly Journal on New Religious Movements* reports that Paul Twitchell of Eckankar borrowed liberally from Julian Johnson's *The Path of the Masters* to frame his new religion.[26]

Preachers Plagiarize Too

King James of England was so outraged by the plagiarism of preachers that he made a law requiring preachers to give at least one original sermon a month.[27] The nineteenth-century preacher Sydney Smith was recognized, "so far as his sermons are concerned … [as] an unblushing plagiarist."[28] Some preachers did not mind accusations of plagiarism. The following limerick was laughingly repeated:

> There once was a preacher named Spurgey
> No lover was he of liturgy;
> His sermons are fine,
> I use them as mine;
> And so do most of the clergy.[29]

Nineteenth-century preaching professor John A. Broadus loathed books of sermons and called them "an unmitigated evil, and a disgrace to the ministry of the gospel."[30]

Is Broadus right? Why should we be upset by preachers using other preachers' sermons? Congregations expect their preachers to produce their own sermons. This has not always been the practice among preachers, as the list of plagiarism interlopers looms large. Among some of the more notable purloined sermons, Peter Marshall's "Compromise in Egypt" looks similar to A. W. Pink's sermon by the same name.[31] Martin Luther King Jr. is widely known for taking titles, concepts, phrases, and paragraphs from sermons of others, and even plagiarized large portions of his doctoral thesis.[32] Some of the more noted plagiarism cases include evangelist Jimmy Swaggart, who was accused of plagiarizing from Dake's Study Bible.[33] In October 2001, Clayton, Missouri Presbyterian pastor Reverend W. Banwell "Barney" Heyward Jr. admitted to plagiarizing the sermons of Reverend Tim Keller of New York City's Redeemer Church. As a result, he lost his job.[34]

Another case of plagiarism hit the press in early 2003, when the Reverend Ed Mullins of Christ Church Cranbrook in suburban Detroit was suspended for ninety days for plagiarism.[35] Later in 2003 came the confession of plagiarism by Washington DC pastor and moderator of the Christian Church (Disciples of Christ), Alvin O'Neal Jackson. Jackson, pastor of National City Christian Church, "used 16 sermons of Thomas K. Tewell, pastor of Fifth Avenue Presbyterian Church in New York, and one by John M. Buchanan, co-pastor of Fourth Presbyterian Church of Chicago, without crediting them."[36]

Then came the case in April 2004, when Robert C. Hamm of Keene United Church of Christ in Keene, New Hampshire, resigned as senior pastor after admitting he plagiarized sermons. "He had taken entire sermons from the Internet and presented them as his own," the church council president Carl A. H. Allen said. "He was very forthcoming and clear that it was an improper thing to do. He asked for forgiveness."[37] Also in 2004, the Reverend Glenn Wagner, pastor of Calvary Church in Charlotte, North Carolina, suddenly resigned after admitting that he had plagiarized sermons for over two years.[38] Reverend Donald Cameron of Providence, Rhode Island, even plagiarized his candidating sermon in addition to the sermons he preached after he assumed the pastorate, until he was caught and then compelled to resign.[39]

Plotting Plagiarism

The history of plagiarism is sordid and long. Plagiarism and cheating pops up in every field and line of employment. People will falsify their resumes, go so far as to brag about receiving a military medal they never actually earned, or even preach someone else's sermon.[40] If we simply looked at the seedy saga of plagiarism, we might be tempted to want to give up and let it have its way. We could count it as one of the consequences of sin and move on. It is not seen as a serious transgression by everyone — and that is exactly when it becomes more elusive, more gray, more hideous.

PLAGIARISM IS A PROBLEM FOR SOME, BUT NOT FOR EVERYONE

Even if plagiarism is a problem, the attitudes about plagiarism vary. They seem even more mixed, especially in the secular world. "What's important is getting ahead," says Alice Newhall, a seventeen-year-old senior at a Virginia high school. "The better grades you have, the better the school you get into, the better you're going to do in life. And if you learn to cut corners to do that, you're going to save yourself time and energy. In the real world, that's what's going to be going on. The better you do, that's what shows. It's not how moral you were in getting there."[41] For this high school student — and for many of us — the end justifies the means.

This pragmatic approach to the practice of plagiarism is not limited to a brazen high school senior. Law scholar and federal judge Richard Posner has a surprisingly similar understanding of plagiarism. Posner admits that plagiarism is "difficult to define."[42] As for plagiarism in his profession, he says that "originality is not highly prized in law."[43]

Posner indicates that since the legal profession functions in a way that cuts and pastes legal opinions, every other field ought to follow suit. However, the opinions given by a judge — with the help of a host of clerks, lawyers, and students — are not subject to the laws of plagiarism. The field of law recognizes that in the process of legal decisions, originality in authorship is not highly valued. Therefore, the substance of the writing of a judge's decision cannot be compared to other works. If the legal profession were to be more forthright, a judge would list the coauthors on the cover sheet of his opinion, or at the very least, include an acknowledgment section citing those who contributed to the opinion.

Posner recognizes the intent of the plagiarizer—to deceive readers, listeners, and viewers into thinking that which was presented was his own but is not—is a serious problem, but nothing more.[44] He notes, "The stigma of plagiarism seems never to fade completely, not because it is an essentially heinous offense but because it is embarrassingly second rate; its practitioners are pathetic, almost ridiculous."[45]

At the heart of Posner's case is whether the plagiarist intended to harm anyone by his plagiarism, indicating that only by discovery of the plagiarism would anyone be harmed.[46] How odd to think that plagiarism is inappropriate only when one is caught. If this is true, what about more serious infractions like abuse or murder? Are they problematic only when they are discovered? Posner's pragmatism certainly raises questions about the definition of plagiarism. His "the end justifies the means" approach is a specter of many would-be and practicing plagiarists.

Remember the accusations of plagiarism waged against Mark Twain? He eventually wrote Oliver Wendall Holmes and asked for his forgiveness (for the presumed plagiarism) and in the letter wrote the following:

> [I] implored him in impassioned language to believe that I never intended to commit this crime, and was unaware that I had committed it until I was confronted with the awful evidence. I have lost his answer. I could better have afforded to lose an uncle. Of these I had a surplus, many of them of no real value to me, but that letter was beyond price, beyond uncledom and unsparable. In it Doctor Holmes laughed the kindest and healingest laugh over the whole matter and at considerable length and in happy phrase assured me that there was no crime in unconscious plagiarism; that I committed it every day, that he committed it every day, that every man alive on the earth who writes or speaks commits it every day and not merely once or twice but every time he opens his mouth; that all our phrasings are spiritualized shadows cast multitudinously from our readings; that no happy phrase of ours is ever quite original with us; there is nothing of our

own in it except some slight change born of our temperament, character, environment, teachings and associations; that this slight change differentiates it from another man's manner of saying it, stamps it with our special style and makes it our own for the time being; all the rest of it being old, moldy, antique and smelling of the breath of a thousand generations of them that have passed it over their teeth before![47]

Reflecting on journalistic plagiarism, *Denver Post* editorial page editor, Chuck Green, says, "I don't think there's anything like a misdemeanor." He continues, "All plagiarism is felonious, but there are degrees of felonies."[48] Malcolm Gladwell of the *New Yorker* is comfortable with more of a free exchange of ideas, rather than worry about plagiarism. He writes, "Creative property, [Lawrence] Lessing reminds us, has many lives — the newspaper arrives at our door, it becomes part of the archive of human knowledge, then it wraps fish. And, by the time ideas pass into their third and fourth lives, we lose track of where they are going."[49] Harry T. Whitin, editor of the *Worcester* [Massachusetts] *Telegram & Gazette*, disagrees. When a star reporter from the newspaper plagiarized from *Sports Illustrated* and passed the work off as his own, Whitin stated, "He broke our compact with our readers."[50]

As for preaching, one historian states that wholesale borrowing of others' sermons "was not disapproved when it was done with skill, and when the ideas of words taken from another were used with success. The literary offence lay in the ignorance and incapacity displayed when stolen knowledge was improperly applied."[51]

"Augustine recognized that some were better theologians and writers than others and that those not good at preparing sermons should preach the sermons of others."[52] He said, in effect, that it is morally right to preach another preacher's sermon, "provided the preacher reproduces accurately what the author has originated and provided that the preacher lives up to what the sermon teaches."[53] One of the reforms of Gregory the Great's mass included the reading of sermons by the Fathers and other great teachers of the church.[54] Likewise, in the eighth century, the plagiarism of sermons was not considered to be a severe problem. For example, Alcuin of York "instructed overworked and underdeveloped priests to utilize the homiletic offerings available to them from the sermons of Augustine, Ambrose, Gregory the Great, and Bede." Alcuin's *Homiliary* was a book of sermons that busy priests could preach from every Sunday. He considered preaching "a duty obligatory for every priest"; however, "it was not demanded he should always write his own sermons."[55]

This same attitude was shared in the Middle Ages. One of the sermon collections that spread over Europe was sold under the title *Sermones Dormi Secur*, which means "Sleep Well Sermons." The preface reflects the attitude:

> Here happily begin the Sunday Sermons with expositions of the Gospels through the year, quite well known and useful to all priests, pastors, and chaplains, which also are called by the other title of Sleep Well, or Sleep without Care, for this reason, that without much study they may be appropriated and preached to the people.[56]

Even Luther instructed his young preachers to read from their pulpits the sermons he wrote; however, he still wanted them to work with the text.[57]

Preaching the sermons of others became popular in seventeenth-century England. John Donne Jr. published a collection of his father's sermons in 1661. He wanted preachers and people to benefit from his father's sermons, saying that "the Churches should be furnished with good preachers, but these preachers should have good sermons."[58] Queen Elizabeth I required that preaching be done by the reading of homilies produced by the hierarchy and distributed to local pastors.[59] Eighteenth-century British Bishop William Paley boldly noted, "As to preaching, if your situation requires a sermon every Sunday, make one and steal five."[60]

The eminent Samuel Johnson wrote sermons for sale. Webb Garrison remarks, "Milton became so alarmed that he denounced 'the multitude of sermons ready printed and piled up, on every text that is not difficult.'"[61]

Even wise Benjamin Franklin was not shaken by a preacher's plagiarism. Philadelphia Presbyterian pastor Samuel Hemphill often plagiarized his sermons. Franklin, who frequented his church and enjoyed listening to him preach, remarked, "I rather approved his giving us good sermons composed by others, than bad ones of his own manufacture; though the latter was the practice of our common teachers."[62]

Not everyone agrees that Franklin has wisdom on this matter. Early twentieth-century preacher and scholar William Gowan asserted, "As long as we put up with men who cannot make their own sermons, and do not protest against them, so long shall we continue to have them."[63]

Philadelphia Presbyterian preacher Donald Gray Barnhouse is known to have a different perspective. An apologetic pastor confessed to Barnhouse that he had been preaching the sermons from his book on Romans. "Young man," said Barnhouse. "You don't have to apologize. That's why we write books. Better that they hear my good content than your stray ideas."[64] Barnhouse's words sound similar to Luther's or to the leaders of the Church of England centuries ago who instructed preachers to copy *their* sermons.

William H. Willimon, although aware of the dangers of plagiarism, comments, "In the Christian church all pastors are colleagues, working together to proclaim the Word to God's people. I fear that some of our contemporary definitions of plagiarism are more capitalist than Christian. They make everything, even ideas about God, into a marketable commodity."[65] Willimon has a point, which we will take up later.

Sam Fulwood acknowledges the point about sharing when he says, "To be sure, black preachers have a long tradition of listening to one another and 'borrowing' phrases, gestures and other congregation-pleasing rhetorical tricks without giving credit. And nobody, including ripped-off ministers, dares think of it as plagiarism." He continues, "So, too, with black entertainers. Rap and house music are derivative arts, featuring heavily sampled tracks from other artists and sometimes mixing various media and recorded and spoken words to create new messages for audiences that are often unfamiliar with the original tracks." But he states,

"Where King and other black ministers might be forgiven in the name of social uplift for their appropriations, no such excuse flows to commercial artists. Some black artists have gone too far and have been challenged for it."[66]

A contemporary Jewish rabbi asks, "Should clergy members be kneeling in their confessionals begging for forgiveness for their sin of plagiarism? I think not, although some churches feel otherwise."[67] Willard A. Pleuthner, a New York public relations executive, asserts that preachers with lesser gifts should adapt and preach in their own words sermons written by others with greater gifts.[68]

In the Mullins case in suburban Detroit, opinion was divided. One member of the congregation stated, "If plagiarism of the sort that Ed Mullins is accused of is punishable, there would be no one preaching on Sunday."[69] Other church members disagreed, "We aren't talking about borrowing an anecdote or idea or two, or even a few well-turned sentences. Mullins is accused of appropriating parts of sermons and articles prepared by others. At worst this is theft; at best it is lying. To say that 'everybody does it' is no excuse, even if it were true."[70]

David S. Blanchard offers a sympathetic pastor's perspective to the Mullins case: "I suspect that most clergy have a degree of empathy with the Rev. Edward Mullins. When it's midnight on a Saturday night and the sermon is not finished most of us will settle for secondhand inspiration over no inspiration at all. And so will our congregations."[71]

After surveying the various attitudes toward plagiarism, there is no solid agreement on the severity. No matter what field of study or occupation, attitudes toward plagiarism vary.

THE LONG-LINGERING RELATIONSHIP OF PREACHERS AND PLAGIARISM

One might expect a laissez-faire attitude about plagiarism from people other than the clergy, but a sermon-stealing preacher seems plain wrong. Joseph Gowan, in his 1922 work on preaching, comments about the permissive attitude toward preaching the sermons of others:

> It may have been permissible for Augustine to take up this attitude, but surely conditions have changed since he wrote these words. What was at one time permissible would no longer be tolerated; and surely the Church requires more competent ministers, in this enlightened age, than those that Augustine proposed to help in this way.[72]

Gowan describes the disagreement at the beginning of the eighteenth century between Bishop George Bull and Bishop Thomas Sprat over the advice given by each to neophyte preachers. Bull advises:

> I give this further advice, that they should not at first trust to their own compositions, but furnish themselves with store of the best sermons that have been published by the learned divines of our Church. These they should read often and study to imitate them, and in time they will attain to a habit of good preaching themselves. Among the printed sermons, those of the late Archbishop Tillotson are well known by all.

Bishop Sprat of Rochester disagreed:

> Every person who undertakes this great employment, should make it a matter of religion and conscience, to preach nothing but what is the product of his own study, and of his own composing. . . . Whereas this sordid borrowing, this shameful I had almost said sacrilegious, purloining from other men's labours, is an utterly irreconcilable enemy to all manner of growth and improvement in divine learning or eloquence.[73]

A similar debate on plagiarism and preaching is tracked in *The Admonition Controversy* between a Mr. Cartwright and a Mr. Whitgift:

> Cartwright (R): I deny that . . . he that readeth another man's sermon preacheth; and further, I say that, if there be any such, as, being able to preach for his knowledge, yet for fault either of utterance or memory cannot do it but by reading that which he hath written, it is not convenient that he should be a minister in the church.
>
> Whitgift (D): And why doth not "he which readeth another man's sermon preach" as well as he doth when he readeth his own? What if he

pronounce another man's sermon in the pulpit without book, doth he not preach because it is not his own? I do not speak this to defend any such ignorant pastor that should need so to depend upon other men's labours; I do but put a case. It may be that a learned pastor having both "memory and utterance" sometime upon occasion may read a sermon. And I nothing doubt but in so doing he preacheth.[74]

Richard Lischer would agree with Whitgift. He assesses Martin Luther King Jr.'s plagiarism in this way: "From the perspective of the church's historic practice, to say that Martin Luther King Jr. received (or borrowed) the words of others and built upon them in response to the demands of the historical moment is to say a very good thing about him. We should all be so unoriginal."[75]

When essayist Charles Lamb was asked how he got his material, he quipped that he had milked three hundred cows for it, but the butter was his own.[76] Lamb's definition is a fair one to consider. "Preparation doesn't mean clicking print or ripping it out of a magazine and carrying it to the pulpit with you," said Steve May, who edits a sermon-sharing website, sermonnotes.com. "The real problem with that [is it] indicates the guy isn't spending time in the Word himself."[77]

About sermon resource sites, Clayton Schmit of Fuller Theological Seminary comments, "These resources can be a shortcut for a busy pastor, but the downside is that a sermon for a general audience cannot address the needs of a local congregation as well as the local pastor can."[78] We will discuss these matters later.

THE END OF THE MATTER

So what are we to make of this leviathan called plagiarism? We may agree with the nineteenth-century humorist who wrote:

Such is a sermon, the whole confusedly dark,
Join Hoadly, Sharp, South, Sherlock, Wake, and Clarke.
So eggs of different parishes will run
To batter, when you beat six yolks to one;
So six bright chymic liquors, if you mix,
In one dark shadow vanish all the six.[79]

We come to the conclusion, as we started this chapter, that the history of plagiarism in preaching is long and the attitudes toward plagiarism in preaching vary.

THINK ABOUT IT

1. What did you learn about plagiarism and what surprised you?
2. What challenges do preachers face as they are confronted with plagiarism?
3. What questions do you have as you consider the topic of preaching and plagiarism?
4. If you are a preacher, what are the specific issues of plagiarism you wrestle with as you prepare your sermons?

THREE

GIVE ME A DEFINITION, PLEASE!

Plagiarism is a subject on which it is often difficult
to say where right ends and wrong begins.[1]

—Joseph Gowan

I'VE SEEN HIM

Have you seen plagiarism before? Do you know what it looks like? Can you describe it? Can you look at his contours and discern his beautiful ugliness? This practice of plagiarism in preaching is a difficult animal to define. Previously, I told you that I had seen and smelled this thing called plagiarism. It is not a pretty sight, for it takes over preachers' lives to the exclusion of their giftedness.

When bank tellers are being trained, they handle all sorts of paper money. They become familiar with it, understanding its touch and texture. Just by feeling the bills, they know a real one from a fake. Perhaps this is what we want to do — to discern plagiarism so we can see it for what it really is — a fake.

Doing this is not easy. As we discussed earlier, there are blurred lines between what is and is not plagiarism. Sometimes the texture of the counterfeit is nuanced to the point that a forgery is almost undetectable. But begin we must.

DEFINE IT, PREACHER

Before we discuss the definitions of plagiarism in preaching, we need to consider the issue of originality, the problem of publication,

There Are No New Ideas under the Sun

Thousands of years of history have made us who we are today — in our thinking and living. Joseph Gowan makes this observation: "'Originality' is not such an easy matter as some would have us suppose. There are not many men who could go out like Columbus, and discover a 'New World'; and even Columbus could not have done what he did, if others had not prepared the way for him, and made the feat possible."[2]

"From a perusal of the literature of the last five hundred years," remarks J. M. Driver, "it would appear that originality, in the absolute sense, is a thing wholly of the past."[3]

The type of originality that we produce as preachers is more of a "third-hand" originality, as coined by John W. Etter. He writes, "The originality which enters mostly into our sermons is third-handed, and consists of our own, or other men's ideas, appropriated to ourselves by a process of mental digestion and assimilation, and expressed in words and methods of our own. This does not forbid, but encourages, the reading of other men's thoughts."[4] Driver calls this "combinative originality." He says, "Ours is to be the originality of treatment, of combination, of presentation, of application of what is already existent and at our command. Nor is this sort of originality to be depreciated. It is really the highest sort."[5]

As preachers, we work to engage our third-hand originality or, as Major General J. G. Harbord, former chairman of the board of the RCA, defined originality, "the ability to put two things together, not to make a third thing equal to the sum of the other two, but superior to the sum."[6] R. W. Dale also offers helpful guidelines for preachers:

> If you want to be an original preacher, look at heaven and hell, life and death, sin and holiness, with your own eyes. Listen for yourselves to the voice of God; ask Him to reveal to you the glory of His love, the steadfastness of His truth, the energy of His righteousness, and tell the world what you have heard and seen. Pierce to the heart of things. Get at the facts which lie behind appearances. In this way originality will come to you when you are not seeking it.[7]

Yet, in some cultures and subcultures, preaching others' sermons is considered to be an expression of honor and an act of respect. Tom Long observes that in some African-American churches and some white Appalachian churches, preachers often do familiar "set piece" sermons, such as "Jesus' Funeral" or "The Deck of Cards"—"a sermon in which the preacher symbolically deals out cards, one at a time, making a biblical allusion for each." Long notes, "The preaching of such sermons is folk performance art, and originality of composition is not the issue. Many of the hearers would have heard these sermons time and again and, as in the case of hearing a jazz riff, would be interested mainly in how the performer improvises on the old material."[8]

One defender of sermon stealing described a particular case of plagiarism.

> At a seminar, Dr. Cho, pastor of the world's largest church in Korea, was asked during a question and answer time, "How do you put your weekly messages together? They are so powerful!" He said, "Honestly, I have never given an original message in all my years of ministry here at Yoido Church. Each week, I preach word-for-word messages from either Billy Graham or W. A. Criswell from Dallas First Baptist Church. I can't afford to not have a home run each weekend when we gather. I don't trust my own ability to give completely original messages."[9]

Of course, Pastor Cho is known for his prayer ministry more than his preaching.

Using others' sermons may be the practice of some in Korea—and other cultures as well—but overall, preaching someone's sermon or using illustrations as your own without giving credit is not considered to be ethical.[10] One difficulty faced by these Korean preachers is that the sermons don't translate well to Korean culture. That's certainly one good reason not to plagiarize! Jung Young Lee notes:

> In almost all Korean preaching, however, I have discovered that most life stories are taken from the West. . . . When I went to hear one of the most respected Korean preachers, a man who is well informed in Korean literature, I had expected to hear sermons based on the life stories of well-known Koreans. However, I was disappointed because his sermons were illustrated

with the life stories of Western people such as Thomas Kepler, Pablo Casals, Samuel Leibowitz, Horatio Nelson, Winston Churchill, Dwight Moody, Francis Parkman, Julio Iglesias, Dorothy Day, and others, and actors, scientists, theologians, politicians, and ordinary persons.[11]

Lee suggests a likely explanation why Korean preachers take from the West: "My suspicion is that most Korean preachers use sermon preparation materials which are written in English when they prepare their sermons.... We need to do some homework to find more illustrative materials from Korean cultural resources."[12]

Kenton Anderson has this advice: "Preachers do stand on the shoulders of others. It is a good practice, for instance, to benefit from concepts, commentary, or even sermon constructions offered by others. In some of these cases, the ideas are essentially in the public domain and no longer need to be cited. In other cases, where either the ideas are unique to a particular source or where the use is substantial, we will want to identify who it is that we have benefited from."[13]

The Light and the Shadow

Because we stand on the shoulders of those before us, we read and soak in all that they produced. Mark Twain describes what happens when we become so familiar with something that we assume we thought of it first. After having read "to rags" Holmes's book on poetry, he writes:

> *Here we have an exhibition of what repetition can do when persisted in daily and hourly over a considerable stretch of time, where one is merely reading for entertainment, without thought or intention of preserving in the memory that which is read. It is a process which in the course of years dries all the juice out of a familiar verse of Scripture, leaving nothing but a sapless husk behind. In that case you at least know the origin of the husk, but in the case in point I apparently preserved the husk but presently forgot when it came. It lay lost in some dim corner of my memory a year or two, then came forward when I needed a dedication and was promptly mistaken by me as a child of my own happy fancy.*[14]

When Twain wrote to Holmes to apologize for his alleged plagiarism, Holmes replied that he too recycled other people's thoughts![15]

"All literary men are subject to what may be called unconscious reminiscences," observes Methodist preacher Henry J. Fox in a treatise on plagiarism. "They cannot always be conscious of the source of their own thoughts. The warp may be their own—in form and fact self-originated—but the woof may be a contribution from the ample, well-filled storehouse of memory."[16] George Sweazey also notes, "There is an anonymous mass of ideas from the common warehouse of humanity. There are stories, proverbs, humor, felicitous expressions, folk wisdom which no one would ever think you were claiming as your own."[17]

These writers and preachers raise the important issue of modeling. Most preachers have pulpit heroes, men or women after whom they model their preaching style. The style might be sermon construction or manner of expression. Modeling one's preaching or writing after another is acceptable, but when it comes to copying directly from another or, as Peter Shaw calls it, "borrowing," it is plagiarism and therefore unacceptable.[18]

The Publication Problem

With the invention of the printing press came the solidification of ideas on paper. As we have seen, books and sermons and all manner of literature were printed—and plagiarized. Webb Garrison notes, "Modern copyright laws, enacted late in the nineteenth century, gradually brought an end to the open theft and sale of religious discourses. Meanwhile, the literary conscience had become much more sensitive. By 1900, it was generally acknowledged that extensive use of another person's ideas and/or language, without permission or acknowledgement, is best described by the blunt word, *theft*."[19]

Richard Lischer has some harsh words for both the nervous plagiarist and the finger-pointing plagiarism police: "Countering the historic practice of the church, the modern appeal to individual genius and the invocation of copyright laws trivializes the tradition and makes it something to be *borrowed* rather than *received*."[20]

We live within the limitations of copyright laws. The tension we face as we resource our sermons is not easy, but it calls for wisdom and responsibility.

Defining the Demon

We can now reach a conclusion to the issue of defining plagiarism. Haddon Robinson states it clearly, "Plagiarism is stealing other people's material. In the world of scholarship, when things are put in print, any idea taken from someone else must be credited in a footnote. In a world of preaching, a pastor who takes sermons from other preachers — word for word — without giving credit is guilty of plagiarism. That is stealing what is not yours."[21]

One journalist defines plagiarism as "the purloining of ideas or language from another source."[22] Another says, "Plagiarism is borrowing someone else's words and passing them off as one's own, whether in print, in speech or performance."[23]

If we were to give a catchy definition of plagiarism, to state it clearly for ourselves and for our congregation, it might go something like this: Plagiarism is a perversion that pounces on other preacher's products and preaches the product as their own personal possession, a profound pollution of preacher and people.

Plagiarism is kidnapping someone else's thoughts, words, or ideas. The practice of it is stealthlike. As discussed earlier, there are realities to the world in which we preach: there is nothing new under the sun; there are lights and shadows along the way, making the defining of plagiarism more difficult than we ever expected it to be; and living under the authority of the law is our obligation. But outright plagiarism is stealing. It is a perversion. It is the seething animal that must be named.

WHAT PLAGIARISM IS NOT

If we know what plagiarism is, then what can we say that plagiarism in preaching is not?

Lack of originality is not a motivation, an excuse, or a definition of plagiarism. Raymond Bailey agrees, "Lack of originality is not plagiarism. Preachers would be better off not to struggle to be original when the possible result may be obscurity or, worse, a distortion of Christian theology."[24] Woodrow Kroll similarly notes, "A person is self-deceived if he denies himself the fruits of other's labors. This should not be the case. His own thoughts may be shallow or even incorrect. He needs the wisdom which God has given to others."[25]

Some preachers treat plagiarism almost like a high school or college guy treats the rules for physical touch while dating. The guy might ask, "Is it okay that we hold hands? Is it okay for me to put my arm around her when we walk? How about when we sit, is it okay then? What about kissing? Can I kiss her on the cheek or on the lips?" The questions all seem to ask, "How far is too far?" A preacher could raise questions like the following:

> If you purchase a sermon or receive permission from the source to use it (Rick Warren says, use my stuff), should you still give credit? If you illustrate from a Time article but get the illustration idea from Joe Stowell, do you credit Stowell? What if you use only another sermon's "angle," its interesting approach to a subject? Or only one of three main points? What if you base your sermon on insights from a commentary?[26]

In the area of preaching and plagiarism, these are good questions, but they may be the inappropriate questions to ask. The heart of the matter is more than rules and limitations. There are more virtuous concerns to worry about than going "too far." Plagiarism in preaching is not defined by a lack of originality, nor is it defined by following the rules. Instead, as we will see in the next section, plagiarism has less to do with actions than with attitude. It has everything to do with taking responsibility.

PLAGIARISM AS RESPONSIBILITY: AN ETHIC FOR PREACHING

All the complicated layers of plagiarism have led us to the point of determining an ethic for preaching and plagiarism. Preachers live in a world of accumulated knowledge, whose availability increases daily. The Internet and the innumerable advances in information technology, in addition to the typical tools and resources available to preachers, provide an incredible temptation for them to succumb to the siren of plagiarism.

An ethic for plagiarism calls preachers to think in at least two ways: about others and about themselves. A preacher's relationship with his or her congregation calls for trust—this is what it means to think about others. In addition, a preacher is asked to consider his or her motives—this is what it means to think about themselves. Both ways of thinking lead us to our responsibility to God.

A Betrayal of Trust

Listeners expect preachers to do their work. They have an unwritten agreement, a covenant, established by themselves and the congregation. As Wiest and Smith observe, "A preacher who violates this covenant by plagiarizing is falsifying the relationship of pastor and people and failing to meet the needs of the people."[27] One pastor wrote to his congregation after confessing to plagiarism, "I cannot yet know how deeply this betrayal of your trust affects you, and can only imagine the hurt that it causes."[28]

Preachers have to maintain a trust with God, their congregation, and themselves. Says nineteenth-century preacher Arthur S. Hoyt, "No language of others, however appropriate and beautiful, can satisfy the ethics of the true preacher. It is not simply the question of plagiarism in its ordinary sense, getting the credit that belongs to another; it is primarily the question of being true to one's self. The words of others are not truly your words."[29]

John Broadus puts it forcefully, "The people do not merely come to hear a discourse—they come to hear a living man, communicating to them his earnest thought and feeling; and if the principal ideas of a sermon are from another preacher, they regard themselves as only hearing a dead man."[30]

One preacher confessed, "I am soon to retire, and looking back upon preaching the gospel for more than forty years, I still find the task difficult. Therefore, I've chosen to borrow heavily from other preachers' sermons." Almost flagrantly he defends himself, "Do I feel bad about finishing my career with sermons based on someone else's idea? Not at all."[31] Maybe he should. Eugene Lowry calls such "borrowing" a widespread form of "deception."[32] One of the responsibilities a preacher has is not to betray a listener's trust.

Misguided Motives

Raymond Bailey pinpoints the motive behind plagiarism: "Plagiarism is the willful representing of the ideas and words of another as one's own. Deceit is intentional, and the motivation is usually personal gain of money or acclaim."[33]

Haddon Robinson agrees, "Motives and honesty are the key issues" in preaching.[34] Eugene Lowry affirms, "When we substitute purchased sermons for that personal reflection, we betray people's time and trust and our own integrity."[35] Preachers want to feed their congregation with spiritual nourishment. However, if feeding them comes at the expense of his personal integrity, then, even if his motives are noble, the plagiarism is deceitful.

That is often where the rub comes for a preacher. The ultimate goal is good, but misguided motives may deter the navigation process. The plagiarism is willful and the preacher defrauds himself and deludes others. We want to mind our motives.

A Reason for Responsibility

"If my regular sermon preparation consists of going online and getting a sermon from somebody else and preaching as is, that is an ethical problem," declares Haddon Robinson.[36] Kenton Anderson says, "Plagiarism is a particular concern for the truthfulness of the preacher. While many would suggest that the pulpit allows latitude in the use of other people's ideas, unauthorized, uncredited appropriation of intellectual property is theft. Plagiarism occurs whenever we pass along someone else's idea or words as if they were our own."[37]

If, as our handy definition states, plagiarism in preaching is a perversion that pounces on other preacher's products and preaches the product as their own personal possession, a profound pollution of preacher and people, then the matter of plagiarism is really more a matter of personal responsibility. We preachers have the individual responsibility to avoid any involvement in plagiarism.

We already established that plagiarism is not a lack of originality or the following of certain rules, although there are guidelines.

I want to suggest that the issue is more than rules and has everything to do with God-given responsibility.

I can point to various nuances of what it means to plagiarize, but we might become pharisaical nonplagiarists. We would pride ourselves on not being plagiarists—not copying this, not borrowing that. We would look at the limits of the rules, but miss the spirit of the rules.

What is the spirit of not plagiarizing? It is a biblical principle from Luke 12:48, "From everyone who has been given much, much will be demanded." This principle is the foundation of not only the issue of plagiarism, but each pastor's entire ministry. The context of the passage is a parable about Jesus' return and how his servants are to live and act as they await him. Jesus is looking for faithful servants who will be honest, genuine, and diligent. That is what an ethic of plagiarism is about—being responsible with the gifts God has given us. We are to be faithful stewards. Plagiarism in preaching is the squandering of gifts that God gives to each preacher. That is why this poison of plagiarism can be so damning to a person's life and ministry. It may not ever reveal itself, it may be jokingly spoken of, or it may be revealed and one's reputation inside and outside of the church may be destroyed. Worst of all, as we will soon note, we displease God.

The attitudes vary, but the reality of its damage is obvious. It seeps into a preacher's study and causes, as my friend Haddon Robinson says, "a curvature of the soul." Why? Because we have been irresponsible, unfaithful—and we put into jeopardy our own spiritual lives. We not only harm ourselves, but we have the potential to harm others, our congregation, even our family.

The preacher who has had the privilege of college and seminary has the responsibility to use the training she received as she prepares her sermons. The same goes for the lay preacher who has studied God's Word. He too has the responsibility to do his best to produce a sermon for the next Sunday. The seminary student who is beginning to put into place the habits of study and preparation has a responsibility to study well now, to ready herself for the future, to determine that she will be faithful and diligent in her classroom preparation and her sermon preparation.

The ethic of preaching and plagiarism, this thing called sermon-stealing, is clear to each stage of the ministerial profession: "From everyone who has been given much, much will be demanded." If you are not faithful in the least of the tasks, you will be judged to be unable to handle the larger tasks. If we do not take personal responsibility for our actions as preachers, then we are truly sinning.

Our ethic is one of responsibility. Plagiarism in preaching is the squandering of gifts that God gives to each preacher. We are responsible to ourselves, others, and God.

PLAGIARISM AS SIN

George Sweazey states boldly: "Plagiarism … is the theft of other people's brainchildren. It is an insidious sin because it is not easy to identify."[38] Not only do we sin against ourselves and others, but also against God. "All sin has first and finally, a Godward force," says Cornelius Plantinga. "Let us say that a sin is any act—any thought, desire, emotion, word, or deed—or its particular absence, that displeases God and deserves blame."[39]

We sin against God and others when we neglect our responsibility as faithful servants to preach the whole counsel of God as the result of our work and study. When we willfully venture into the territory of pushing the limits or breaking the rules of plagiarism, we have sinned. If we are honest with ourselves, we will recognize that we sinned well before we copied an outline, borrowed an illustration, or preached someone else's sermon. We sinned when we ignored our responsibility to use God's gifts to do his work.

Disturbingly, the sin of plagiarism may only be the presenting problem in a person's troubled soul. The infection in our souls may be more grave and disconcerting. As Plantinga observes, "The reason [for this] is that sin distorts our character, a central feature of our very humanity. Sin corrupts powerful human capacities—thought, emotion, speech, and act—so that they become centers of attack on others or defection or neglect."[40] Plagiarism may hide even the seven deadly sins (pride, sloth, envy, anger, greed, gluttony, and lust). "We know that when we sin, we pervert, adulterate, and destroy good things," says Plantinga. And when we do, "we involve ourselves deeply in what theologians call corruption."[41]

Plagiarism is sin. We have named it, and we know how tempted we are by it. But we are called to a higher calling of being responsible servants to a loving Lord.

THINK ABOUT IT

1. How is plagiarism in preaching defined in this chapter? Do you agree with this definition? Why or why not?
2. How do you react to plagiarism as sin?
3. If you are a preacher, as you prepare your sermons, in what ways are you most tempted to cheat?
4. How do you respond to the idea that "from everyone who has been given much, much will be demanded"?

CHAPTER

FOUR

INTEGRITY IN PLAGIARISM AND PREACHING

Mutual cheating is the foundation of society.
—*Blaise Pascal*

INTEGRITY IN A CUT-AND-PASTE WORLD

A few years ago, a colleague in the ministry was caught plagiarizing sermons from a nationally known preacher. A few members in his congregation called him out. At first he denied it, but later he tearfully confessed that he was guilty of plagiarism. Soon after the incident, I shared with him my interest in interviewing him for this project. He cheerfully agreed. However, when I later contacted him, he said he had changed his mind, insisting that the accusations were unfounded and that he did not want to be interviewed.

I do not know if this pastor had ever come to terms with the weight of the situation. Tensions were high in the church. Several members left. His preaching ministry was suspect. Somewhere along the way, he found himself unwilling to accept his responsibility to himself, the congregation, and God.

How are preachers able to preach with integrity in a cut-and-paste world? How can preachers give sermons responsibly and avoid inner conflicts and tension with God? Can it be that preachers are not focusing on their primary responsibility?

Mark Taylor suggests that "the church needs a leader, an evangelist, a counselor, a servant, and a manager every bit as much as it needs a public speaker. If a minister can do well at even two or three of the first five, can't we cut him some slack on number six?"[1] The question still remains, what is the pastor's job? What is the responsibility of the pastor?

Preachers are being lured away from their primary role as pastor to that of visionary or CEO, transforming the model for pastoral ministry from pastor to executive, or even an entertainer and motivational speaker. This shift gives less emphasis on preaching — and its preparation. Preachers are now required to encourage congregants to give to the capital campaign, to provide direction on how to live life, and to challenge listeners' attitudes toward any number of social issues. All of these are important, but not as important as the primary task of the preacher, the pastor. We are neglecting our own souls.[2]

"Three pastoral acts are so basic, so critical, that they determine the shape of everything else," says Eugene Peterson. "The acts are praying, reading Scripture, and giving spiritual direction."[3] When preachers veer away from the center of ministry, it puts everything else off-kilter as well. The way pastors lead their lives serves as a message to others of God's redemption through Christ. As David Hansen notes, as a pastor, "my employer is Jesus Christ. Serving the church is my obedient response to Christ. Jesus is my boss: he orders my day. Shivering while preparing my sermons forced me to take seriously who I was preparing my sermons for: Jesus Christ — who also had no place to rest his elbows. The church got better sermons because of it."[4]

Eugene Peterson writes through satire about the dismal state of the ministry. Because the priorities of many in pastoral ministry today are so out of focus, he suggests that it would be easy to train any person with minimal education to be a pastor "who would be satisfactory to any discriminating American congregation." He jokingly suggests a curriculum that includes "Voice Control for Prayer and Counseling," "Efficient Office Management," "Image Projection," and the most damning for our purposes, "Creative Plagiarism." On "Creative Plagiarism" Peterson hits close to home when he suggests, "I would put you in touch with a wide range of excellent and inspirational talks, show you how to alter them just enough to obscure their origins, and get you a reputation for wit and wisdom."[5] Sadly, Peterson's satire contains a lot of the truth of plagiarism.

Preachers, church boards, and congregations need to recalibrate their perceptions and understanding about the nature and substance of pastoral ministry. We will then see again pastors who are preachers of integrity, for they have returned to the priorities of what it means to be a pastor. As Hansen observes, "The pastoral ministry cannot be employer-driven, trend-driven or task-driven. Pastoral ministry must be following Jesus Christ. Jesus Christ called me to this work, and following him must be integral to realizing his calling."[6]

PREACHING SERMONS WITH INTEGRITY

Integrity in preaching begins by being responsible in the preparation of our sermons and rethinking our role as a pastor and preacher. The pastor's study can be an isolated place. Responsible preachers need to practice honesty with themselves, others, and God. Here are some steps pastors can take to guard themselves against plagiarism.

We Can Be Honest with Ourselves

When preparing our sermons, we want to be brutally honest with ourselves. What steps are we going to take to prevent plagiarism? Are we willing to be vigilant in maintaining standards of truthfulness as we prepare to preach? Remember, in sermon writing, we are not asking the "how far is too far?" questions. Instead, we need to press ourselves with the question, "Am I being responsible with the gifts God has given me as I prepare this sermon?"

Plagiarizing sermons may indicate other deeper problems. "Sermon stealing usually appears to be a symptom of other problems in a preacher's life," Cary Dunlap observes. "If you're 'taking' from other preachers more than you know you should, take a closer look at your life." His advice: "Don't ignore the problems or hope everything will come out okay in the wash. Get it now."[7]

We Can Be Honest with Others

Our connectedness is underscored by our relationship to our congregation. Depending on your church structure, you may already have a line of accountability where you can test your questions and therefore strengthen your integrity. Haddon Robinson advises, "In the cases where we use most of someone else's material, it would be wise to discuss this with church leadership. They ought to be part of our conscience, understand why we want to do this, and agree to it."[8]

When we are honest with the wider church body, we demonstrate that we are exercising the responsibility God has given us.

We Are to Be Honest with God

In our lonely work in the study, we are reminded of our responsibility before God. Honest study begins with an open relationship with the living God. Begin your study of God's Word with prayer, and trust his Holy Spirit to lead you to what you will need to communicate his Word to your people. If while you study your will is flagging, ask God for his help. When you feel you cannot make sense of the text or know how you will preach it, plead with God for his guidance and strength.

A host of resources are available for study. And as we plow through them, we can trust God to help us be responsible with the gifts he has given us. Jamie Buckingham puts it this way, "Everything we say is free, and we expect nothing in return. Everything we borrow we try to give credit — not because credit is due, but because God has a way of blessing honesty."[9]

When we approach our task with honesty — with self, others, and God — we gain an appreciation for the incredible task we have before us as preachers. It is a responsibility that God will help us accomplish with integrity.

WHY DO WE PLAGIARIZE?

Preaching with responsibility and integrity means that we are aware of our own predispositions, who we are personally, and how our inclinations and even our excuses affect us as preachers.

We are sinners. Not one of us reading this book will deny this reality — or you would not be worried about the sin of plagiarism! We are made up of twisted sinfulness that leads us in directions of which we may or may not be aware. The hymn writer was right when he penned these words: "Prone to wander, Lord, I feel it, / Prone to leave the God I love."[10]

The following are possible paths to plagiarism. They are conditions in our own thinking and living that indicate possible weaknesses that might predispose us to sermon stealing.

Unreflective or Unexamined Self-Awareness

We are too often isolated as pastors. We are viewed as the spiritual leader but have few colleagues or friends with whom we can be open and accountable. What is worse, although we might have a steady prayer life and regular nourishment from God's Word, we still may lack the ability to be self-reflective. What do I mean by self-reflective? Few of us really know our strengths, our weaknesses, or even our motivations. Often times we do things socially or relationally that we may not be aware of, or have even thought about. We get in our own way. If we really knew ourselves, if we were self-reflective, we might be able to avoid some of the difficulties we face in our lives. We want and we need to know ourselves. We need to be self-reflective, self-aware. We desire an examined heart. Once we know ourselves, we can accept responsibility and act with integrity.

After his ministry came crashing down following accusations of plagiarism, one pastor admitted that he felt his life was out of control, that he was in "a downward spiral, emotionally and mentally, which left me very tired and discouraged and fighting a losing battle with depression."[11] At the time all of this was happening, he was not able to do anything about it. He lacked self-reflection and a network of support.

Insecurity

Some of you might have had a similar experience to Haddon Robinson when he compared himself with other preachers. While he was in seminary he heard the stellar preachers of the day: Harry Ironside, Vernon McGee, Roy Aldrich, Stephen Olford, and Ray Stedman. "After hearing these preachers, others were inspired," says Robinson. "But I walked out of the service wanting to quit."[12]

One of my friends has a saying, "Comparison is the thief of joy."[13] I think he is right. When we measure ourselves against others, we will always be disappointed. Comparing ourselves to others steals the pleasure of preaching. We can certainly learn from our contemporaries, our peers, and our mentors, but we will never become them. When we find that we do not or cannot measure up, we give up as we are overtaken by our own perceived inadequacies.

My word of advice: don't do it! Once we start believing our fears, we will be tempted to steal from others. You *can* preach. You *can* do it. Do what you have been trained to do. Be responsible with your gifts.

Laziness

As a young pastor, I remember one of the first visits by my area minister. He was the pastor to the pastors in the area I served. Claude asked me how I was adjusting to being a pastor. I told him that I loved it and was doing what God had called me to do. During the course of the conversation, Claude said something to me that I have never forgotten. He said, "Scott, do you know who are some of the laziest people I know?" He answered himself, "Pastors."

Over the years I have met many diligent, responsible pastors. I have also met lazy pastors who are not only physically lazy, but also intellectually lazy. The two seem to converge and produce a pastor who wants to be pastored rather than being pastor himself. Woodrow Kroll describes how an intellectually lazy pastor may be characterized, "This type of preacher never thinks for himself. He never cracks his

Greek text. He never even reads the portion of Scripture which he has selected for Sunday's message until he reads a commentary. His whole life is wrapped up in what others have said. His sermons are one long quote after another."[14] Inadequate preparation will reveal slovenly exegesis, application, and even eisegesis.[15]

In addition to being physically and intellectually lazy, all too often preachers—who should be the opposite—might be spiritually lazy as well. Laziness—in all forms—may well be the propensity of a preacher on the edge of plagiarizing.

Need to Compete

One of the problems that plagues our culture, says Stephen Carter of Yale, is that "we care far more about winning than about playing by the rules."[16] That is the case with some preachers who are in perceived competition with other preachers. They may vie as to who the better preacher is consciously or unconsciously. They want to impress, no matter what it takes—even if it means copying from others. This attitude views preaching as a performance—that preaching is all about us, the preacher. The desire to impress may be heightened by perceived expectations from one's congregation. The key is to check our motives. Why do we do what we do? When we are in the spotlight, when the sermon is the center of the service, we start thinking it is about us. Allow me to assure you, it is not about you.

Like the apostle Paul, most of us do not preach "with eloquence or superior wisdom." But, we can echo Paul's words, "For I resolved to know nothing while I was with you except Jesus Christ and him crucified. I came to you in weakness and fear, and with much trembling. My message and my preaching were not with wise and persuasive words, but with a demonstration of the Spirit's power, so that your faith might not rest on men's wisdom, but on God's power."[17] Paul did not want to compete against the orators of his day, and we don't either.

Loss of Morale

Ministry is tough. It is easy to get discouraged. Pastors contend with matters that the average person could never imagine: spiritual conflict, relational disappointments, discipleship setbacks, family crises, and personality tensions, among others. Sometimes there is not a lot of encouragement in ministry.

I remember one preacher telling me that as he shook hands at the door on Sunday morning one of the members of the congregation handed him a slip of paper listing the grammatical errors he made in the sermon. She did this weekly. After this the kind words from others fell flat on the floor.

It is little wonder that pastors plagiarize. Still, the low level of encouragement in the pastorate is no excuse to plunder another preacher's sermon. In light of this, however, one can appreciate the burden under which pastors serve.

Out of Focus

Misplaced priorities can lead to overcommitment, undue busyness, concern about our public selves and our public reputation, and burnout. "It is much more challenging to deliver a sermon than to develop the person who preaches it," says Eugene Peterson. "It is far more stimulating to organize and administer a parish program crisply than to live for weeks or months in uncertainty waiting patiently for clarity for vision."[18] The preacher's priorities are to pray, to be both a student and teacher of God's Word, and to disciple others. One pastor reminds us that "pastors forget what their primary calling is."[19]

Responsible preachers know themselves and are ready to refocus their pastoral priorities. When this happens, they are able to guard against weaknesses that may lead one to plagiarize.

EXCUSES FOR PLAGIARIZING

Many of us are good at excuses. We have doctorates in excuse making. The following are some possible excuses preachers use in order to legitimize why they plagiarize.

I'm Too Busy So I Have to Plagiarize

Some preachers will excuse their plagiarism because they are too busy. One pastor confessed that he was too busy doing other things to focus on sermon preparation, "My ministry is most effective when I sit down with two or three men in a restaurant and talk about how to serve Christ and build his church." He admitted, "Exegesis and homiletic skills are frankly not my forte." His sermon preparation was characterized by plagiaristic borrowing.[20]

About busyness in the pastorate, James W. Cox comments:

Unfortunately many ministers welcome interruptions and multiplied parish duties: These things offer plausible and justifiable escape from the discipline of study and sermon preparation; they also offer a ready excuse for Saturday night plagiarism. However, on this, ministers are both sinning and sinned against. Their hectic activity and going in circles may be the result of their failure to organize efficiently the time available to them.[21]

"I have heard colleagues try to excuse their stealing an entire sermon by saying that they were too busy to write a sermon and had no other choice. Rubbish," says one preacher. "All one need do is get into the pulpit and say, 'I had five funerals this week and had no time to do justice to a sermon. However, here is a really good one of William Willimon's that I would like to share with you.'" She continues, "Being too busy to write a new sermon is not a sin. Pretending we have written a new one when we have not is."[22]

Preachers make many choices. However, they have a priority to choose study—the systematic study of God's Word in preparation for preaching.

I'm Not Educated So I Have to Plagiarize

During his later years as a pastor, Billy Graham was asked what in his life he would have done differently. He responded that he would have gotten more schooling.[23] Whatever schooling a preacher has or does not have, he or she has the responsibility to do his or her best to prepare to preach.[24] You may be intimidated by others' skill and ability, but if God has called you to preach, you are to prepare with diligence, not borrow with delight.

Take advantage of training in preaching and biblical studies. There are numerous opportunities for study through distance learning and the Internet. Your task is to become better at what you do and take the steps necessary to do it. Use whatever education you have to its fullest. When you do, you will be acting responsibly, avoiding the pitfall of plagiarism.

I'm Not That Clever So I Have to Plagiarize

When we start comparing ourselves with others, we will potentially paralyze our own effectiveness. A pastor might lament, "I can't seem to hit home runs in my sermons like Chuck Swindoll does. If I preach his sermons, maybe I'll see the results I want to see in my preaching." Such thinking is self-deceptive. This preacher's feelings of inadequacy due to comparison derailed his thinking and mixed his motives. Instead of being vigilant, he is taken off guard by focusing on himself and not on the God who has equipped him with his gifts, allowing the temptation of plagiarism to take over.

Another kind of problem arises when the preacher delivers a sermon or gives an illustration as if it happened to him. Wayne Harvey notes, "Telling half-true or untrue stories to our congregations can threaten our integrity."[25] As noted in chapter 1, in my reading group, one of our number confronted the preacher at the door about a story he had told. We almost got booted out of the church!

This kind of plagiarism also comes in the form of taking on the characteristics and cadences of another preacher, perhaps nationally known or locally respected. But the unreflective preacher who compares himself with the other and finds himself wanting may partake in plagiarism. He talks, walks, gestures, and generally imitates the great preacher. He is not himself. Daniel Kidder warns against this homiletical habit: "But when we seek to imitate other men's intonations, forms of expression, and modes of thought, we to a certain degree become plagiarists, and are generally rewarded according to our deed by only succeeding to imitate the faults rather than the excellencies of those we admire."[26]

Darryl Dash faced the same problem. He attended a seminar led by a preacher whose sermons are on the Internet. The seminar changed the way he preached, but he said his sermons "sounded a little like his." As he started using other people's sermons, "I was open with my leaders that I consulted other people's sermons as I prepared my own. But—and here is the problem—I was sounding less and less like myself, and more and more like some other preacher. I was losing my own identity. In short, I was selling out."[27]

Phillips Brooks' definition of preaching is an ample guard against this pitfall. Brooks defines preaching as "truth through personality." The personality is to be uniquely yours, no one else's. While sermon stealing is literary plagiarism, A. J. Gordon calls this kind of plagiarism "moral plagiarism," which, he says, "is worse."[28] Karl Barth reflected, "Preachers often have a model in mind. Nevertheless, they must put *themselves* into the pulpit, for *they* are the ones who are called."[29]

One old preacher sums it up this way, "In short, be not Simpsonized, nor Spurgeonized, not Chalmerized, but Emmanuelized."[30]

WE CAN PREACH SERMONS WITH INTEGRITY BY BEING ON GUARD AGAINST PLAGIARISM

In order to guard against falling into the grip of plagiarism, responsible preachers are to defend themselves on several fronts.

Be Vigilant by Studying Responsibly

Nothing can replace the hard work of exegesis and study. The shortcuts offered by websites or published sermons pale to the connections a preacher can personally make from the Bible to his or her congregation.

Pastors study groups, lectionary sermon work groups, and even congregational sermon or worship-planning teams can help.[31] However, they should not take the place of diligent study on the part of the preacher. We can guard against plagiarism by doing our own work. This does not mean that we do not consult commentaries, histories, and other resources. Responsible preachers should put sermons together "the old fashioned way."

Martin Luther valued study, railing against preachers who don't do their homework:

Some pastors [rely on commentaries] and other good books to get a sermon out of them. They do not pray; they do not study; they do not read; they do not search the Scripture. It is just as if there were no need to read the Bible for this purpose. They use such books as offer them homiletical helps in order to earn their yearly living; they are nothing but parrots and jackdaws, which learn to repeat without understanding, though our purpose and the purpose of these theologians is to direct preachers to Scriptures.[32]

What does this mean? If you have been trained in the original languages, you have a responsibility to use them—and your congregation will expect it too. Brandon Cash contends that regular engagement in the study of the original language of the Bible will help reduce plagiarism: "When pastors quit engaging the biblical languages they begin to rely solely on the writings of others for their studies."[33] As for the congregation, Andrew Blackwood observes, "As a rule they wish him to preach messages distinctly his own. Since he has gone through college and seminary, and has six days every week between Sundays, he ought not to appear publicly in used garments, even if they have come from a metropolitan preacher."[34]

Let the Point of the Text Point to You

In the rush to prepare a sermon for the following Sunday, we tend to think of the listeners—what they need to hear, what they ought to hear, and what we want them to hear. However, in the routine of preparing the sermon for our listeners, we forget ourselves. We ignore that we come under the authority of the same text the congregation will hear. Haddon Robinson's definition of biblical preaching captures the mandate of the text over preachers:

Expository preaching is the communication of a biblical concept, derived from and transmitted through a historical, grammatical, and literary study of a passage in its context, which the Holy Spirit first applies to the personality and experience of the preacher, then through the preacher, applies to the hearers.[35]

Notice the phrase "which the Holy Spirit first applies to the personality and experience of the preacher." The preacher is in the same position as those to whom she preaches—under the authority of the biblical text. The truth of the text is to be applied to the preacher. We often miss this in our mad dash to sermon preparation.

Self-examination in preachers was a trademark of New England Puritan preaching. "Before calling the congregation to account to God for their lives, thoughts, and feelings," notes Harry Stout, "the minister first had to submit his own life to a withering divine scrutiny. Only then could he project that message outward and say to his congregation with the proper combination of humility and finality, 'Thus saith the Lord.'"[36]

Preachers are to bow to the same truth of the text that they are asking their listeners to submit to. When we let the text direct us, we will be better able to proclaim it with sympathy, love, and conviction.

Read Widely and Take Notes

It almost goes unnoticed, but the preacher is constantly on the search for material for future sermons. That is why the preacher needs to have his finger on the pulse of newspapers, news magazines, popular culture, and electronic media. Webb Garrison suggests, "A high level of productivity demands an even greater rate of intake. For ministers, this means reading widely and making careful use of some system of taking notes."[37]

Reading widely is common advice given by teachers of preaching and other preachers. Mike Graves suggests that one of the reasons preachers plagiarize is that they have neglected reading: "They read their Bibles and the sermons of others, but maybe not enough literature—Emily Dickinson, John Steinbeck, Kathleen Norris, Frederick Buechner."[38] William Willimon observes, "We Christians try to be dependent on the thoughts of the saints. Creativity, particularly Christian creativity, is not a lonely, heroic, individualistic achievement."[39]

When we broaden ourselves by reading newspapers, news magazines, novels, and short stories, or even listening to stimulating radio or watching movies, we expand our thinking. When we widen our world, our preaching will be different. We will be different. Responsible preachers have an eye on the written and wider culture.

Give Credit

"Few congregations will think less of a minister who frankly states that the outline of a sermon was adapted from Wesley, or one of the major points from Spurgeon," said Webb Garrison in 1952. "Failure to make such acknowledgement is a way of claiming complete originality. And when a supposedly original sermon is found in a book, the minister does indeed descend in the estimation of his people."[40]

What was true in the 1950s is true today. Haddon Robinson observes,

> When we make someone else's ideas our own, the line between what is 'original' (nothing is truly original) and what is plagiarized is difficult to discern. But clearly if we take most of our material for a sermon from another preacher, then it is a matter of honesty and integrity that we give credit. . . . When we use someone else's sermon outline, one way we can easily give credit is "I came across an approach to a sermon by so-and-so, and I want to share it with you."[41]

Eugene L. Lowry agrees, "When the preacher has borrowed the gist of the text's meaning or a decisive sermonic turn from another's work, it is easy to note this in the bulletin: 'I am indebted to my colleague the Rev. Neighbor for this helpful insight regarding today's sermonic theme'; or 'Thanks goes to Dr. Homiletician for clarifying the gospel lesson for today.' Alternately, the preacher might acknowledge another's assistance just before the reading of the biblical text, or at some other time in the service prior to the sermon."[42]

Oral footnoting can sound clunky. Am I required to say, "Brothers and sisters, this next thought comes from Richard Pervo, who in a 1997 article published in the *Journal of Biblical Literature* writes"? I agree with Mike Graves in saying, "No, thanks!"[43]

Baptist preacher John Broadus advises, "Avoid a parade of honesty about acknowledging."[44] Preachers would agree with Jamie Buckingham when he states, "Most speakers hate to break the flow in the middle of a message. It's much easier to keep going than to confuse the hearer with a score of footnotes plugged into the actual text.... But courtesy calls for gratefulness—as long as it can be given without distraction."[45]

If a preacher shaped the sermon along the lines of someone else, he can give credit in the bulletin instead of a verbal acknowledgment, especially if an outline or additional material for the sermon is published regularly.

There are always nagging questions when preachers prepare sermons. "I came up with this insight into the text on my own, but then I read the same thing later in Stott. Should I give him credit?" You probably don't have to, but citing Stott would certainly bolster your argument, showing that you think the same on this matter as a leading theologian.

Suppose your big idea is worded the same as, say, a sentence you read in one of Kent Hughes's books. Do you say where you got it from? Again, it's not going to clog up the sermon if you say, "Kent Hughes puts it this way" and then comment, "That's how I'd say it too."

If you use an illustration that you've read but don't remember which book, and you've heard it in any number of sermons, do you give credit? I'm not advocating that sermons are term papers, but I am pushing for responsibility. There's no harm in citing where you got the illustration, but are you being honest in your preaching when citing other sources?[46]

There are no doubt a host of other questions readers might have, but the principle of this book should not be crowded by our questions.

One pastor learned the hard lesson of using another preacher's sermon—and he got caught: "Keep your motives pure, and communicate truth by making your sources clear."[47] That is a good, but tough lesson to learn. Responsible preachers give credit where they should—but don't name drop either.[48]

SERMON WEBSITES AND PREACHING HELPS

As we have noted in our brief study, sermon helps have been part of the church for centuries. All of them raise questions about the preacher's responsibility to self, others, and God. Questions about the validity of these resources continue. "What about those sermon sets one can buy, the ones that now even follow the lectionary?" asks Eugene Lowry. "You don't even have to copy them. Some provide a wide margin on the right side for any comments one might want to add. The preparers intend pastors to preach them." But he notes, "While not plagiarism, using these sermons is thievery of another kind."[49] He continues:

> When we substitute purchased sermons for that personal reflection, we betray people's time and trust and our own integrity. It would be more honest to have the real writer tape [audio recording] the text, and to play that tape for the congregation. For the pastor to present someone else's sermon as if it were the result of his or her own discipleship, training and theological commitment is to bear false witness.[50]

"We recognize that a sermon is different than an academic paper or a novel," says a sermon database editor. "The goal is not to earn a doctorate, it's to serve the church universal. We're trying to help not with original words, but with the word of God."[51] The editor's statement is unclear, but one thing is certain: someone is benefiting from online sermon services, and it might not be God.

Perhaps the greatest issue with websites and preaching helps is that they can short-circuit a preacher's responsible preparation for his or her sermons. An editor of a sermon-sharing website observes, "The real problem with that [is it] indicates the guy isn't spending time in the Word himself."[52] But another website flagrantly disagrees, "It's OK to borrow from others' sermon manuscripts," the website states, "as inspired preaching cannot and should not be copyrighted." The reporter of the story reflects, "If all this leaves you nervous, you're not alone. Preachers surfing for inspiration worries me, too. There's a risk of outright plagiarism, of course. But a subtler danger is at work — pastors choosing to take a shortcut to a sermon rather than putting in the effort that a congregation has a right to expect of its spiritual guide."[53]

Do these resources help or inhibit creativity and study? Lugene Schemper says, "Sermons on the web are no substitute for the hard work that goes into imaginative, sound biblical preaching, but when used properly they can be an aid to the preacher's development and spiritual growth."[54] However, Andrew Blackwood states that preachers should avoid any of these aids. His stern warning from the 1950s would no doubt be stronger today. He states, "Give no shelf room to books of sermons outlines or canned illustrations, even if they come from Spurgeon or some recent master. Do the same with homiletical commentaries, which deprive the preacher of lasting joy in using his intellectual muscle."[55]

What is the bottom line when it comes to these and other resources? A responsible preacher does the majority of his or her own work, possibly stimulated by various preaching resources, and prays to God for wisdom, guidance, and discernment.

AVOID THE PARASITE OF PLAGIARISM

To sum up all that we have covered, we will do well to heed the words of John Broadus:

> It is certainly important that on the whole subject of borrowing, one should have just principles; and that he should early in life establish such principles, and form correct habits from the beginning. Otherwise, there will either be a wrong practice continued through life, with very injurious results to a man's character and influence, or, when he comes to see more clearly, there will be much to regret in his past course.[56]

"Preachers are like comedians," says Richard Lischer. "They're always looking for new material."[57] Preachers can preach with integrity in a cut-and-paste world by recognizing their responsibility as preachers to themselves, others, and God. Then and only then will they be able to avoid the parasite of plagiarism. We will mess up, but we have a God of grace who uses our weaknesses to bring him glory. Ultimately, that is what we want to do, give God all the glory.

THINK ABOUT IT

1. Do you think there is a shift in the focus in your ministry or that of your church? What are ways you or your congregation can recalibrate to assist your preaching and service as a pastor?

2. In what ways do you relate to the reasons why preachers plagiarize?
3. Review the excuses for plagiarizing. Do you see yourself or anyone on your church staff in any of them?
4. How can preachers intentionally guard against plagiarizing others' sermons?

FIVE

PREACHING IN A
CUT-AND-PASTE WORLD

Some pastors [rely on commentaries] and other good books to get a sermon out of them.... They use such books as offer them homiletical helps in order to earn their yearly living; they are nothing but parrots and jackdaws, which learn to repeat without understanding.

—*Martin Luther*

AVOIDING THE CLUTCHES OF PLAGIARISM

We are coming to the end. I want to emphasize that I do not write this book with negative prejudices toward preachers. I am a preacher myself and preach almost weekly. I served churches as a pastor and preacher. I teach neophyte preachers and work with experienced preachers. I have a lot invested in all these folks and in you. I do not think that most preachers are lazy people, liars, and general no-goods. Instead, I believe preachers have a high calling, a noble task, to communicate God's Word to men and women and boys and girls. My desire is to call pastors to a higher level of preaching, to consider the matter of plagiarism and either put to death its effect on us, or at least provide suggestions to avoid its clutches.

CAUGHT IN THE WEB

As we discovered, the opportunity for a preacher to kidnap another preacher's stuff has been readily available for centuries.

Whether it is a book of sermon outlines, sermon transcripts, a published sermon series, or any number of web resources, the thoughtful preacher has to be discerning and diligent.

The motives of those who offer various sermon resources are certainly magnanimous. They want to help preachers and, in turn, help the preachers' congregations. The desire to help is praiseworthy and at first blush, innocent. The goal of one megachurch in providing sermon transcripts is "to help other pastors kick-start their own creativity."[1]

The responsibility with the use of the material, say the sources, is with the user, the preacher. One church leader says, "We realized that we had several years' worth of sermons already transcribed, so why not make these available as a potential resource in a pastor's toolbox? Needless to say, we're trusting that the pastor on the receiving end is exercising integrity and solid character in how they're using the content and how it is being presented to the congregation."[2]

The resources on the web are immense and can be helpful. However, as Craig Webb of LifeWay Christian Resources notes, "Recently, there has been a development where preachers have become sermon editors rather than sermon writers. Preachers feel inadequate with so many good resources available. In fact, the abundance and the use of those resources becomes like an addiction replacing good preparation."[3]

It's true that the preacher has the responsibility to use appropriately the sermon material made available in its various forms. However, is it not also true that the provider of the material also bears some responsibility for making the material available in the first place? I am not trying to pull an Adam here — "she made me do it" — but I want all parties to share in the responsibility of what is done.

Of course, the motives of putting material in books, magazines, or on the web will vary. Evangelicals tend to be marketers; they know how to pitch what they sell or, in this case, preach.[4] The resource of Pastor So-and-So may help you to preach like him. As a result, Pastor So-and-So's influence is broadened by preachers using his material and he also has the potential to benefit financially.[5]

One preaching resource magazine provides material that "is unsigned by design." Personalities are diminished. The author explains, "We provide the corn; we expect you to grind it in your own mill.... And we don't care whether you give us credit or not."[6] This can be confusing for the thoughtful preacher.

Websites on preaching are a source for many preachers as they put together their sermons, but they may unwittingly cloud the matter of plagiarism. Although they appear to be a healthy attempt to help preachers, one might suspect that the websites are sometimes driven more by the winds of the marketplace. Materials are presented to help preachers, but the effect of this help is rarely considered. As ministry ethicists Joe Trull and James Carter note, "The ready availability of sermons on the internet has made the temptation to plagiarize even greater."[7]

When Thomas Long discovered that one of his students had plagiarized a pastor's sermon, he found that not only had the student plagiarized the sermon, but so do many others who post their sermons on the web. Long notes, "With a few clicks of the mouse, I had uncovered a crime wave of homiletical petty larceny."[8]

What are preachers to do with the ever-increasing amount of "resources" available? Richard Lischer files this minority report on the first principle of homiletics: it is not "Be yourself" or "Find your own voice," but "Whose wisdom will help form me as a preacher?"[9] Lischer's statement raises some important questions. Are there guidelines we can follow that will help us to be preachers with integrity in a cut-and-paste world?

Being Original

When we talk about preaching and plagiarism, we are not talking about being completely original. The Scriptures are not original to us, but to the God who gave them. Biblical language research is not original to us either. We use language guides, syntax reference books, dictionaries, commentaries, and a shelf full of reference material that does not come from us. In addition, we have read books, heard lectures, and engaged in conversations that are all part of the forming of ourselves as pastors.

In the past, preachers-in-training were told to avoid going to the commentaries before they did their own exegetical work. Now preachers are warned not to go to the web before they have done their exegesis. One pastor confessed that he does not have a library as he can find everything he needs for research on the web. This is an alarming approach to sermon preparation, let alone an unsettling perspective of what it means to study and engage in research in general.

Be Choosey

To be blunt, not all sermons or sermon series plans that are recorded, printed in a magazine or book, or posted on the Internet are worth preaching. Just because a famous preacher delivered the sermon or designed the series does not mean that the sermon is biblically based, textually sound, or right for your church. Much of what drives publication is reputation. Some of what is published is motivated by ego—a person's desire to be recognized or maybe even financial gain. Not one of us is a home-run hitter all of the time. Not all of what we write or preach is totally on the mark, but too often desperate preachers find solace in using others' material. The propagation of yet another sermon preached from the packaged sermon or sermon series perpetuates poor exegesis, watered-down theology, or misappropriated application.

One pastor said after having looked at other preachers' stuff, "Honestly, sometimes all I glean from them is how not to approach a subject, or that I need to go in a different direction with my study."[10] When examining resources, be choosey, be discerning. Not everything published is good stuff.[11]

Do the Right Thing

As preachers, as men and women of integrity, we really want to do what is right. If we use someone's stuff, Mike Graves advises, "Attribution demands that credit be given where credit is due; contribution demands having something worthwhile to say from one's own life and study. Both are essential to preaching."[12] Of course, there are those who disagree. Some websites consider membership or purchase of materials as giving the preacher free reign to use the material as he or she sees fit. Others ask members to cite their sources. Still others instruct pastors, "If my bullet fits your gun, then shoot it," and don't bother giving me credit for it. Why? "They are preaching a sermon, not footnoting a term paper."[13] To be safe, give recognition. You'll be glad you did.[14]

Remember Who's in Charge

No matter the amount of effort we put into preaching, it is God's role to use us as preachers and to help, lead, instruct, or guide our listeners. Preaching is not simply human communication. Nor is it "the fine art of talking in someone else's sleep."[15] Preaching typically finds its place in the midst of worship, for preaching is worship. Preachers recognize that what they do is holy — it is God's. God chooses to use men and women to communicate his will to a world in desperate need of hearing it — and being transformed by it.

We do not preach ourselves. We preach Christ, the gospel, the Scriptures, and the Word of God. Preaching is God's work and we humbly participate in what he's doing in the lives of our listeners.

WHEN TIMES ARE TOUGH

Let's face it; there will be times when you will have three funerals over the course of the week, board meetings, and preparation for Bible study. Somehow Sunday sermon preparation falls off your radar screen. What do you do?

If you use another's sermon, you could state, "This past week was a tough one for me — and for us as a church. In the midst of caring for three families and my other responsibilities, I was not able to prepare as well as I would like and as well as you deserve. However, I do have a sermon for you. It isn't mine, but it was preached by [Preacher X]. What he has to say is important for us to hear this morning. His words are my words to you." Your listeners will appreciate your honesty and will respect you for it.

Still another approach — and perhaps the more preferable — is to give to the congregation what you have prepared. The preface to the sermon may be similar to the one before, but the outcome is completely different: "I was not able to prepare as well as I would like, and as well as you deserve. But I do have a sermon for you and I'd like to show you what the Scriptures have to say to us in light of what we've been through as a church." Your honesty as a person will allow your preaching to go a long way.

Maybe the most sage advice is given by one preacher who adopted this principle: "'No matter how busy I may be this week, it is not an option to get up in the pulpit and inform the congregation that there was no time for a message this week.' So the pressure to produce is continually there as the weekly deadline approaches."[16]

To determine whether something is plagiarism or not is not as difficult as one might think. At least that is what Leslie Holmes believes. He considers plagiarism to be an issue of the heart: "If you know in your heart—and it is a heart issue—that the material you're using in your sermons originated with someone else, you ought to give them credit for it."[17]

WHEN YOU BLOW IT

What are the steps a plagiarizing preacher can take to return to responsible sermon preparation?

Confess

After he was found to have plagiarized, one pastor confessed that his plagiarizing of other's sermons was "wrong." He told his congregation, "It is difficult to admit failure, but I ask for your forgiveness." Another plagiarizing preacher said, "I take full responsibility for what I've done."[18] Confession means takes responsibility. Confession names the sin. Take your punishment or discipline with humility and grace.

Repent

The essence of repentance is change. Repenting requires the changing of one's mind and attitude. In the case of plagiarism, a preacher has to change his mind that his plagiarism was not right, but wrong. It is sin. We have shirked our responsibility as preachers.

Once we confess and repent, we have to be aware that, but for the grace of God, we may do it again. This is the case with authors—"writers who plagiarize tend to do it more than once and sometimes break other literary rules as well."[19] It is the case for preachers as well.[20]

Be Restored

If you have come to terms with your sin, accept the consequences and move on with grace, knowing you have been forgiven. "In short," says Cornelius Plantinga, "we are to become responsible beings: people to whom God can entrust deep and worthy assignments, expecting us to make something significant of them—expecting us to make something significant of our lives."[21] We can be restored in our relationships to others and to God.

Set Up Plagiarism Parameters

So much of what a preacher does to prepare his or her sermons is conducted without oversight. In the case of a plagiarizing preacher on the road to restoration, you will want to set up healing parameters to prevent it from happening again.

Draw a line of accountability. In an age where material is readily available on the web, one pastor states that there is accessibility without accountability.[22] The healing plagiarizer should set up a circle of accountability—a person or a group of individuals who will hold him responsible for his sermon preparation.

One talented pastor told me that after he has completed his sermon exegesis, he checks a major website for sermons on the text on which he has been working. Sometimes, he acknowledges, the sermon he refers to helps him shape his own sermon. Is this an appropriate use of sermon websites? Sure it is—if you acknowledge the help. However, this same pastor remarks, "Sometimes I feel so pressured to get the sermon done that going to the website is almost the lazy thing to do."

This young pastor has the gifts to construct a sermon from which his congregation will benefit greatly. He was helped by the website, which cannot be denied. My discomfort with his story is that he knew that the website was a shortcut. The advice I gave him was this: "You're a gifted preacher. Stay away from the websites and see what you come up with without it." He promised me that he would avoid the website in the preparation of his sermons in the future. He has not turned back. Preachers who short-circuit their abilities would be better served studying and avoiding the Internet—cold turkey.

Prepare in advance. The next bit of advice I gave this young pastor was to prepare his sermons in advance. Devise a sermon plan that provides a healthy biblical diet for his congregation. He should study the congregation to realize its needs and put together a plan that meets those needs.

One can get into a rhythm of not only having a plan, but also beginning preparation for the next week's sermon ahead of time. The preacher could exegete the text for the following week's sermon on Thursday or Friday, some ten days before that sermon is preached.[23] This gives the preacher more simmer time to pray and prepare.

A sermon group may be helpful in sermon preparation. The preacher can select a small group of people from the congregation to meet regularly and lend a hand to the pastor with sermon preparation. Having prepared the biblical study and come up with the sermon idea, the preacher can use the group to fill in the holes. The "huddle" can suggest what yet needs to be explained, provide illustrations, and clarify the preacher's points. Not only will the "huddle" offer creative input, but it may also develop good pastor-to-people relations.[24]

Pray for restoration. Every pastor is in need of prayer. The temptation to plagiarize requires extra spiritual resources of strength to resist. Preachers can enlist prayer partners who will specifically pray for her for the task of sermon preparation. How much more does a repenting plagiarizing preacher want and need prayer for healing and restoration! Sermon preparation is a spiritual act and those who get ready to preach require spiritual support. Recruiting prayer support is critical.

Is a preacher's ministry over if he or she plagiarizes? No, especially if after reading this book you have become convinced that you have been plagiarizing and are willing to follow these parameters. However, if you do plagiarize and get caught, there is a high probability that you will experience public humiliation or even the loss of your ministerial position. The question is not whether or not you will eventually be exposed as a plagiarizer, but whether you are using your gifts and your background to the Lord's honor now.

Get Additional Training

If you are struggling with your preaching or sense that you need help, get more training. You might not have undergraduate education. If you have the ability and the resources—financial help is often available through denominations or churches—get it. Seminary training is not out of reach. Courses are offered on the Internet or you might be within driving distance of a Bible college or seminary. Those who have a Master of Divinity degree might consider enrolling in a Master of Theology in Preaching program or a Doctor of Ministry degree in preaching.

Another way to supplement your preaching education is to attend conferences and workshops on the practice of preaching. In addition, there are numerous audio and video resources from which preachers can benefit.

One layperson observes, "To be an undereducated preacher teaches those in the pews that the gift of schooling provided for us by God is not valued, that the Christian education that could be provided to us is not thought to be essential, and that the preacher does not consider it important to engage in personal Christian learning as a lifelong activity."[25]

The bottom line is, powerful preachers are always growing, deepening, and learning what it means to be someone who knows God through his Word and through prayer, as well as knowing God's people and his world. A preacher who does not plagiarize runs deep is his wisdom. Centuries ago Bernard of Clairvaux recognized this when he wrote to pastors:

If . . . you are wise, you will show yourself rather as a reservoir than as a canal. For a canal spreads abroad water as it receives it, but a reservoir waits until it is filled before overflowing, and thus communicates, without loss to itself, its superabundant water. . . . In the Church at present day there are many canals, few reservoirs.[26]

Use Others' Material Responsibly

Sermons are prepared in symphony. Using the sources of the original languages of the text, exegetical tools, commentaries, and other materials, the preacher prepares to preach. If you find that your sermon is being shaped or influenced by another preacher or teacher, give credit: "I learned this from John Stott." Or, "I benefited from the way Warren Weirsbe shaped his sermon on Philippians 2. His work shows up in my sermon today." Or, "One Bible teacher says it this way."

As Tom Long notes, "Giving credit to others is not merely a matter of keeping our ethical noses clean; it is also a part of bearing witness to the gospel."[27] Responsible study leads to responsible preaching. When you honor the work of others, you honor your listeners and the Lord.

Imagine the Consequences

No one wants his or her ministry tainted or ruined. No one longs to be mistrusted or have one's integrity called into question. When a plagiarist is exposed, no one can be certain about the outcome. Researcher on cheating Barbara Mary Johnson urges, "Try to imagine the consequences. Then look at the exact opposite approach. Consider, in either case, who will be hurt and who will be helped."[28]

However, we do not want to avoid plagiarism simply because of what might happen to us — guilt is not the best motivator. There are more people involved in our indiscretions than ourselves. We have a responsibility to be honest with God, others, and ourselves. As Johnson notes, "Basically, caring about other people keeps us from cheating them. Except in unusual circumstances, we don't lie to someone we love. One basic reason for being honest is neighborly love."[29]

"Thinking matters through before we act is always difficult and often consumes a significant part of our time," says Stephen Carter. "But it simply is not possible to be a person of integrity without doing it."[30]

Plagiarism has everything to do with our integrity. It is foolish to not give credit for someone else's work. "Foolishness leads to being a fool," says Keith Phol. "Taking the easy route leads to an empty head. There are three basic ingredients to good preaching: study, prayer/meditation/creative thinking, and sensitivity to our people's world."[31]

Go Back to the Basics

I do not leave this section until last because it is of a lower priority. Instead, I mean for it to be a final instruction, as a closing and weighty exhortation. The life of quiet prayer and study seems distant from the busy lives of pastors today. A fundamental way to guard against sermon plagiarism is to reorient one's ministry to the study of the Word, prayer, and discipleship. This is of the ultimate importance in the battle against plagiarism.

BOARD MATTERS

Church boards or judicatories are often taken by surprise when the charges of plagiarism are waged against their pastor. The loss of confidence in a well-respected pastor or colleague in the ministry can leave a church board or governing body in doubt as to what to do. They know they are not dealing with a sexual moral failure, but they still are confronted with something that can have the same effect on a congregation—a loss of integrity and trust.

Get the Facts

When an accusation of plagiarism is made, the board has the responsibility to get the facts. Our task as spiritual leaders is that of restoration, not retribution. We are prone to think the worst of people rather than the best. We need to remember that even preachers wander and the spiritual leaders are the ones who have the responsibility to bring them back.

Set up a fact-finding committee. Let's say a board member had someone from the congregation confide in him that the pastor has been plagiarizing. What can the board do? Set up a subcommittee. A smaller committee of two to three with the responsibility of reporting to the larger committee may work best in these situations. Pray for the preacher's restoration, for wisdom in the process, and for cooperation by all parties involved, including the congregation. Finally, ask that God lead you in every step.

Get the evidence. The next step is to contact the accuser, who then will provide hard evidence of the plagiarism for the committee to evaluate. Instruct the accuser not to share his or her concerns with anyone else. Plagiarism is a delicate matter and should be kept confidential while the group does its work.

Meet with the accused. Once the accusation has been corroborated and the facts are written out, the committee meets with the preacher. In a loving and respectful manner, the committee members share with the preacher the accusation along with the evidence. If the initial response is denial, the committee is responsible for determining how the preacher actually goes about constructing his or her sermons. When confronted with the evidence, the preacher will need to be given the opportunity to explain himself.

Determine the frequency. If plagiarism has indeed taken place, it's necessary to determine if this was a once-only incident of plagiarism or if this is the preacher's common practice. An "I was too busy with the two funerals I had this week to put a sermon together" answer may suggest that the preacher simply messed up. If plagiarizing sermons is a common practice, then the committee is dealing with a much deeper problem.

Lifestyle plagiarism might suggest other problems than just stealing sermons: has the preacher actually been performing the other pastoral duties? Since the pastor's time is flexible and often unaccounted for, a congregation and governing board assumes that the pastor is doing what he was hired to do—being the shepherd of the flock. After plagiarism, the preacher's integrity is brought into question and creates a breach of trust that sometimes is irreparable. Tom Long notes, "Perhaps as much or more than any other form of communication, preaching depends upon a cord of trust binding together the speaker and the listener, the preacher and hearer."[32]

Dealing with the Situation

Confess the sin. When a preacher plagiarizes, he is saying that what he is preaching is his own and not someone else's. The preacher sins against the Lord, the congregation, and himself. A confession and a claim of repentance by the preacher announced at a regularly scheduled worship service, with the leaders of the church joining him for prayer, can be a powerful redemptive statement.

A carefully worded letter by the pastor and the church leadership sent to the congregation and posted on the church website can also reflect what the preacher stated in the public service. In addition, the pastor and church leadership can outline the steps they are taking for restoration and/or discipline.

Determine the discipline. Churches and judicatories will deal with pastors plagiarizing in different ways. The range of discipline is wide. Some have chosen to discipline the pastor with a leave of absence from all pastoral duties (with or without pay), while other pastors have been fired.

The purpose of discipline is to be redemptive—for the plagiarizing preacher and for the congregation. It's important to be careful, since the guilty preacher may not have the best perspective on what restorative discipline means. Some may not even be totally convinced of the severity of plagiarism and want to suggest a workable program that selfishly suits their needs or goals.

I am aware of preachers who have parlayed a "soft landing" for their infraction. The discipline laid down was innocuous and carelessly implemented. Both the preacher and the congregation were deprived of a spiritually maturing experience. The challenge is to follow through with the discipline, even though it will be difficult for everyone. If time off is necessary, see to it that a period of distance for repentance and healing—for both parties—is done. If more education is needed, get it. If more training is necessary, do it.

Restoration takes time. Church leaders have the responsibility to follow through with the correction. Sin has consequences. Discipline is a process of dealing with the repentance from sin. Repentance does not happen immediately, even with spiritual leaders like pastors. Map out the program of restoration to serve as a covenant between the pastor and church leadership. Appoint the appropriate people to follow through with the preacher on the accepted guidelines. These individuals should report regularly to the larger group over the course of the period of restoration.

In the case of a termination of the plagiarizing preacher, the church leadership will want to determine the best venue for making the announcement public. Be aware that there will be some members of the congregation who will not agree with the decision made by the leadership, nor will they consider plagiarism a severe infraction deserving dismissal. An open forum on the termination of the preacher may provide the occasion for the congregation to grieve and ask questions. This may also be an excellent time for the leadership to pray for the preacher and for the church. Churches are tested in times of difficulty. What better way to chart a positive course for the future than to bring the congregation together in prayer?

Be ready for contingencies. Preachers are public figures. When a preacher plagiarizes, make sure the board's public statements to the congregation and to the press are accurate and fair. No one wants to be represented shoddily. Be prepared for questions from the press. A prepared press release will help diffuse initial questions and will provide an accurate account of what happened. A spokesperson who can be the public "face" for the church may also help with community concerns. This person can be the point of contact who handles queries and provides information to the public.

We live in a litigious age. Boards and judicatories would be wise to have legal counsel on hand in order to gain insight and guidance on these matters. Some boards may want little information shared with the public, while others are comfortable with full disclosure. Whatever the agreement, it needs to be honored and carried out delicately.

Moving On

I remind boards that they are not corporation oversight directors. Rather, they are spiritual leaders, serving together to lead God's church. You have the immense responsibility of spiritual oversight of the church and the pastor. Your task is to keep the pastor focused on the priorities of his or her ministry. As Eugene Peterson notes, "Pastoral work has no integrity unconnected with the angles of prayer, Scripture, and spiritual direction."[33]

The expectation that the pastor should be able to shoulder any number of tasks beyond the trinity of prayer, Scripture, and discipleship, is asking a lot. When a pastor is chief fundraiser, school principal, and building committee chair, among other tasks, his preaching is bound to suffer. You as a board may unwittingly share responsibility in the pastor's spiral into the sin of plagiarism. Work to recalibrate the pastor's responsibilities. Prioritize the essentials so that his preaching reflects his relationship with the Lord and demonstrates integrity.

DENOMINATIONAL DECISIONS

Denominational officials who encounter a plagiarizing preacher can follow the steps toward restoration I suggested. Some additional guidance is found in denominational handbooks on the ethics of plagiarism.[34] Three early twentieth-century codes — the 1926 Methodist Code, the 1927 New York Presbytery Code, and the 1931 Congregational Code of Ethics — appear to share the same source. They serve as model to others when they state, "It is unethical for the minister to use sermon material prepared by another without acknowledging the source from which it comes."[35]

Some modern codes condemn the practice of plagiarism while others ignore it completely.[36] As one ministerial ethicist notes, "All ministerial codes and ministers everywhere condemn plagiarism, though they recognize that everyone is indebted to those who have spoken or written before them and that often the thoughts and minds of the great leaders of the Christian pulpit must, per-force, be followed."[37]

Typically, the decision regarding the plagiarizer's ordination credentials is addressed at the denominational level. Whether it is the local church or at the regional or synod level, the appropriate committees will require the information garnered from the church board inquiry. Depending on a given church's relationship with its judicatory, the denomination may have been called in at the beginning of the inquiry. Each denomination has its own process for dealing with pastoral failings. Nevertheless, a redemptive course is recommended.

CUT AND PASTE

Preaching and plagiarism is not an enjoyable topic. It makes us uncomfortable and uneasy. Preachers are caught pilfering sermons all the time—sometimes even catch themselves. As Stephen Carter notes, "If we happen to do something wrong, we would just as soon have nobody point it out."[38] As servants of the Word we are called to be careful with our words and the words of others. Preachers live in a cut-and-paste world. Yet we are called to be men and women of integrity. To do so is not easy, but worth it. When we fail, we can be restored. We can accept the consequences and move on redemptively, refocusing our lives and ministries on what is most important. When we do, God is glorified.

THINK ABOUT IT

1. In what ways has the Internet caught you or tempted you in your preparation for preaching?
2. What plan do you have to ensure against plagiarism?
3. If you've blown it—whether others know it or not—what have you done or what will you do to redeem yourself and move away from plagiarism?

4. What are the ways that churches (be it local churches, boards, judicatories, or denominations) can help guard against plagiarism?

5. Now that you've completed this book, what is your attitude about preaching and plagiarism? How has it changed, if at all, as a result of reading this primer?

AFTERWORD: KIDNAPPING WORDS

From everyone who has been given much, much
will be demanded.

—Luke 12:48

On a beautiful Sunday morning in summer, Harry Emerson Fosdick greeted a young pastor at the door of a church in coastal Maine. He had just heard his sermon—that is, he had heard the young preacher preach one of Fosdick's own sermons. Fosdick was the last person to greet the preacher at the door. The elderly Fosdick at first demonstrated interest in the sermon. He asked how long it took him to prepare it.

"'Oh, it took me about three hours,' replied the youthful person loftily. 'Young man, that sermon took me twenty-one hours to prepare!' declared the summer visitor, in what became immediately apparent as a full-pulpit voice, frequently broadcast over the radio. 'Well, Dr. Fosdick,' replied the parson with charming brass, 'You keep writing 'em and I'll keep preaching 'em!'"[1]

British preacher William Sangster had a similar experience. While on vacation, he made his way to an evening worship service. The pastor picked the same text Sangster had preached on three or so weeks before. His introduction was exactly the same as Sangster's too. He remembered, "Word for word my sermon came out—just as it had appeared in a verbatim report from a religious journal which had published it without permission. The central illustration was a personal experience of mine. He gave it as his own. My children sitting beside me in the pew remembered the sermon and looked at me in astonishment. I blushed for the cloth. If I had been preaching in that pulpit a week later and had repeated my sermon, *I* should have been suspected of plagiarism."[2]

A grieving daughter relates in a Dear Abby column that she wrote a eulogy upon the sudden death of her elderly mother. The priest required her to submit it to him to determine if it was "appropriate." At the funeral, the preacher, who really did not know the deceased well, used the exact words the daughter had written about her mother. "I was, naturally, taken aback at his using my own heartfelt words, which I had labored over and rehearsed for two days," noted the daughter. "When I was to speak, I was able to recover enough to reference 'Father's' remarks earlier — but it was extremely upsetting to suddenly hear my words coming out of his mouth. I could understand if he had wanted to coordinate his remarks with mine, but he outright stole them." Abby replied, "The priest who plagiarized your eulogy was a thief. He stole your intellectual property to make himself look good at your expense, and he should be ashamed of his laziness."[3]

Here are three people with similar experiences. Their words were kidnapped. Stolen. Fosdick, Sangster, and the grieving daughter found their own plagiarist. Other plagiarists may be outed by someone in their congregation or others who discover the filched sources in magazines, in books, in audio sermons, or on the Internet. Fosdick and Sangster gave their plagiarists a tongue-lashing and the anguished daughter wrote a confronting letter. Plagiarizing preachers have been punished from verbal accusations to firings. Still, some believe that being concerned about plagiarism committed by preachers is "a needless waste of God's momentum."[4]

This is not the case in other fields outside of preaching. Plagiarism is something to be taken seriously, and most preachers do. The concern about plagiarism has spawned the development of devices that spot plagiarism: computer programs, websites, reference books, and handbooks.[5] One can even type out a phrase or a sentence on an internet search engine and find that the copycat's crime will soon be revealed on the computer screen. The prevalence of plagiarism isn't due to ignorance either. In one survey we took on the topic of plagiarism every respondent was able to define what it is.[6] This doesn't stop preachers from pinching sermons.

Who needs preachers, then? Why not use videos or video-feed, piping the sermon into a church, from anywhere?[7] Why not just get people to read a sermon written by someone else? One church-goer disgruntled by sermon-stealing preachers offered this sarcastic solution:

> There is now a wonderful way for churches large and small to save some much needed cash while still enjoying high-quality preaching. I propose that each congregation entrust a group of respected congregants to find that week's sermon on the Internet and then take turns reading it to the congregation. Cut out the middleman! Ministers will object to my proposal, arguing that they do far more than prepare sermons. However, the preparation and delivery of a sermon is still considered to be the primary responsibility of a minister.
>
> Churches could use the money they save for outreach to the poor and needy in their communities or many other worthy endeavors. This would also encourage people in the ministry who aren't capable of preparing sermons to find other lines of work for which they are presumably more qualified.[8]

This little primer is intended to encourage preachers to be faithful with their God-given gifts and to use them to their utmost. When we once again practice the priorities of what it means to be a pastor, we will not lose sight of our responsibilities in preaching, and we will not plagiarize.

When we focus on the results—delivering a sizzling-good sermon, showcasing our skill, or striving to be better than the next preacher—we are drawn away from the ethics of doing what is right, just, and honorable. Jesus' statement to those who have been given responsibilities until his return is a ringing reminder of our responsibility as preachers and to those who support us: "From everyone who has been given much, much will be demanded." Lord, make us faithful.

A CASE STUDY: WHOSE SERMON IS IT?

John V. Tornfelt

Karen McDonald had been blessed profoundly over the past six weeks by Dr. Bill Martin's series "Coping in Crises." She thought his messages had been exceptional. Karen mentioned to friends she believed this series was among his best in the years he had been ministering at Grace Church. Passages were clearly explained, and the applications were appropriate and sensitive. It seemed that Dr. Martin had insights into her life, and Karen offered heartfelt appreciation to him as she left church each Sunday.

Karen was so engaged in the series that while at the Christian bookstore one Saturday afternoon, she purchased a book with a title similar to the series. As she sat at home that evening and thumbed through the book, Karen noticed that the content seemed to strangely resemble Dr. Martin's. Even the stories were similar except for minor details where he may have adjusted accounts to make them sound as if they personally happened to him. As Karen puzzled over her findings she called upstairs to her husband, Andy, to explain the situation. Though he had not been at the church for several weeks because of his work as a professor at the local college, Andy was not initially bothered by Karen's discovery and encouraged her not to jump to any conclusions.

Before heading off to bed, Karen read a few chapters in anticipation of the next day's sermon. She could not get her mind off this troubling coincidence. Throughout the night, she tossed and turned. She remembered the story her mother related about a pastor in a nearby town who was found to be preaching the sermons of others as if they were his own. He was eventually dismissed from his church for this reason.

The next morning, Andy and Karen took their seats in the sanctuary with some apprehension. In fact, this Sunday they sat three rows further back than usual. When she looked in the bulletin and saw the title of the sermon was different than the chapter title, Karen was relieved, even though the message was based on the same text as she had read the night before. However, as Dr. Martin began to preach, Karen realized that last week's sermon was not an isolated incident. Though not an identical copy, it seemed as if parts of what she was hearing came verbatim from the book. She pulled the bulletin from her hymnal and scribbled across the front page, "He's done it again," before slipping it into Andy's hands. Following the postlude, Karen insisted they slip out a side door because of her discomfort with the situation.

As soon as they arrived home, Karen ran upstairs to confirm her suspicions. Though there were some differences, the material was essentially the same. While eating lunch, Karen asked Andy what should be done. She wondered how many sermons had been created in a similar way. Andy recognized his wife's inner conflict as he listened to her stream of questions. "Is this situation a breach of integrity? Does anyone in church recognize what was happening? Should she tell anyone, and if she did, would they believe her? If the pastor was being less than original with his messages, could God still use him to minister? Should she remain in the church?" As Andy patiently listened to Karen's concerns, he was truly at a loss. Though he knew it bothered her greatly, Andy wasn't quite sure what to say.

Karen did not want to hurt Dr. Martin. She had been a member of the church for nine years and had served on the church council with him. She valued his insights and wisdom. He had been especially caring and had ministered to her deeply both after her father passed away two years ago and also during her recent stay in the hospital. Because of these factors, Karen felt both upset and deceived. Though perplexed, the McDonalds decided the proper course of action was to pray about the situation over the next few weeks.

For the next four Sundays, Dr. Martin continued with his series. During the week, the McDonalds read the corresponding chapters. As they listened each Sunday, they became convinced that the sermons had been lifted from the book. Though the pastor explained the passages clearly and illustrated appropriately, the McDonalds now listened in sadness. Finally, Andy had heard enough and said while walking to the car from a service, "Something needs to be done not only for the good of the church but also for Dr. Martin's sake. However, I'm not sure what should be done or how to go about it."

Before heading home, Andy and Karen stopped for lunch at their favorite restaurant. While waiting to be seated, their friends Bill and Janie Hunter and Art and Louise Williamson walked in the door. Since they had not seen each other in a while, they decided to get a table together and "catch up."

After ordering their food Art said, "Boy, wasn't that a great sermon by Dr. Martin? I've been gone for a few weeks on business. I sure miss his preaching when I'm away." Janie echoed Art and commented how Dr. Martin's stories were so personal and relevant. While Bill and Louise nodded their heads in agreement, Andy and Karen were silent.

When Art asked them what they thought of Dr. Martin's sermon, they just looked at each other, unsure of what to say. Andy fiddled with his napkin, and Karen continued to stir her coffee as they tried to respond. Since they had been trusted friends for many years and Karen currently served on the church council with Janie and Art, she figured it was an appropriate time to bring up their concern. Karen looked over to Andy and asked, "Should I tell them?" He shrugged his shoulders and with some reluctance, told her to go ahead.

"Since you asked," Karen said, "over the last several weeks, we've been troubled by something." Smiles turned to shocked looks. "Let me explain our concerns. Some weeks ago, I picked up a book at a Christian bookstore and from what I've read, it appears that Dr. Martin is taking his sermons from it. The content is much the same. Even his stories, though not identical, are like the ones in the book. At times on Sunday, I'm not sure whose story it is — Dr. Martin's or the author's. Sadly, this has not happened just once or twice. As we've looked back over the series, there appears to be a pattern." Then she added, "We are disturbed by the situation. You're the only people whom Andy and I have told. It just doesn't seem right to use someone's materials and claim them as your own. If Andy caught a student at the college doing something like this, it would be called plagiarism and wouldn't be tolerated."

Art was the first to respond. Though he was chair of the church council and was used to hearing complaints and concerns from members, this one was different and far more serious. "I'm more than surprised. I'm shocked. But are you sure? It just seems so out of character for him."

Andy answered, "Yes, we are sure. If you want, you can see the book for yourself. But we're not out to get Dr. Martin. Like you, we love him and appreciate what he has done at Grace Church."

Though he never entered the ministry, Bill had attended seminary and remembered how students were challenged to be authentic, do the research, and preach with conviction. In order for this to occur, it was essential that pastors spend time in God's Word and apply its truth to their own lives before attempting to communicate to their people. He mentioned the old adage, "It can't happen through you until it happens to you," commenting that he still believed it to be a good principle to follow.

Then he added, "I'm not sure why he would do it. It doesn't make sense. He's bright, engaging, and so capable. It just doesn't seem like him. I don't understand why."

Janie wasn't sure anything was really wrong. She countered, "What's so bad about using someone's materials especially if they are good? Besides, how many fresh ideas is Dr. Martin supposed to have? Can you imagine how difficult it must be to come up with something new every Sunday? I know there are all sorts of materials available for ministers to use. They can buy books, get sermons on the Internet, and listen to CDs and audiotapes. What are such resources there for? I bet most ministers use something! If his messages are striking responsive chords in people's lives, shouldn't we be glad that good things are happening?"

After listening to the exchange for a few minutes, Louise turned to the McDonalds and said: "I'm not sure what to think. Just don't make a bigger deal out of this than you have to. We have more important things to deal with than the source of his sermons. Have you considered going directly to Dr. Martin?"

Andy responded, "Louise, I disagree. This issue is important. We've contemplated meeting with him but did not feel it was appropriate quite yet. We have been praying about the situation. After today's sermon, I mentioned to Karen something needed to be done for the good of the church and Dr. Martin. When Art raised the question, we figured it was as good a time as any to talk. You've been our friends for years, and we have done many things together at the church. We are struggling, because we want to do what is best."

Louise offered, "I don't know about everyone else, but I still think you should go see Dr. Martin. Doesn't the Bible say that if you have a problem with someone, you should go to that person?"

Janie disagreed. "I'm not sure what it will achieve. I'm still not convinced that he's doing anything wrong. Besides he might not appreciate your findings. He can get rather angry when things aren't going his way, or someone decides to challenge him on an issue. But don't let me stop you."

While driving home, Andy commented that he agreed with Louise's suggestion. "We need to talk with the pastor." So on Monday morning, he called Dr. Martin and asked if they could meet with him because they had a matter they wanted to discuss. Thursday evenings were a time he normally set aside for such meetings, so they scheduled an appointment.

As the time for their meeting drew closer, Karen reflected on the lunchtime conversation with their friends. Although Janie's words of caution caused Karen to become increasingly nervous, she believed the meeting with Dr. Martin was necessary. The McDonalds arrived promptly at 7:30 and after a few pleasantries, Andy pulled from his pocket a few notes he had jotted down.

Before he had a chance to speak, Karen burst into tears and blurted, "Why are you preaching someone else's sermons and pretending they are yours?"

Dr. Martin acted as if he didn't know what she was talking about and responded, "I'm not sure what you are getting at." Though he was more subdued, Andy was still nervous and uncertain what to do following Karen's outburst. With Dr. Martin's cautious reply, Andy sensed it was an appropriate time to pull out the book from Karen's purse and place it on the desk.

Dr. Martin was shaken by this unexpected confrontation by the McDonalds, people he considered loyal supporters. He drew a deep breath as he mentally scrambled to find words of explanation. When Karen asked again why he was preaching someone else's materials, he defensively stated he was simply borrowing a few ideas and commented how his clergy friends did as well. In fact, he stated how he was aware of only a few pastors who actually wrote their own material.

With a smile on his face, he said, "While playing golf on Monday with my colleagues, we sometimes joke about our sermons and whose message we preached on Sunday. Besides, I am often short on time with so many responsibilities, such as hospital visitations, counseling appointments, and various meetings. Some weeks, it is difficult to find time to prepare."

Dr. Martin tried to rationalize. "Why should I attempt to write a sermon, especially in its entirety, when someone else has already done it better than I could?" When Karen asked him about the integrity of preaching these sermons as if they were his own, he shrugged it off.

"Besides," he said, "I thought you liked my sermons. Didn't you tell me just a few weeks ago how helpful they were for you?"

That night, the McDonalds drove home in silence. Dr. Martin didn't see anything wrong with his actions. Although they understood the burdens he carried as their pastor, they were dismayed by his nonchalant attitude and unwillingness to make changes in his pulpit ministry. When almost home, Karen broke the silence and said, "Maybe Louise was wrong and Janie was right. Perhaps this meeting wasn't such a good idea after all."

The next evening, Art Williamson called to remind Karen of the church council meeting on Monday night. Earlier in the day when Art had met with Dr. Martin to set the agenda, the topic of an upcoming sermon series was discussed. Although Dr. Martin wanted to start next month, Art was a bit hesitant as he recalled their conversation on Sunday. While on the phone, Karen informed Art that they had met with Dr. Martin the previous night and shared her disappointment with the outcome. Not surprisingly, Dr. Martin had not mentioned the meeting to Art.

Although he was unsure how to deal with the matter, Art was convinced the issue should not be ignored and remarked to Karen, "Well, it seems like I have another item to add to the agenda."

TEACHING NOTES ON "WHOSE SERMON IS IT?"

Objectives
- To promote authenticity in preaching.
- To consider the forces which lead individuals to depend on other clergy's work.
- To evaluate the effects of plagiarism in the construction of sermons.
- To seek ways how preachers can maintain integrity while benefiting from the efforts and insights of other communicators.

Issues
Personal: What issues may Dr. Martin be facing that are contributing to his extensive use of another person's material?

Biblical: What biblical principles apply to this situation? How can this issue be handled in a godly manner?

Leadership: How should church leaders respond as they learn of Dr. Martin's actions?

Congregational: What are the long-term effects on the congregation if Dr. Martin continues with this practice?

Characters

Primary

- Dr. Bill Martin
- Karen McDonald
- Andy McDonald

Secondary

- Art and Louise Williamson
- Bill and Janie Hunter
- Clergy golfing partners

Teaching Plan

Entry questions (10 minutes)

1. How unique or widespread do you think situations like this are in our churches?
2. Can you recall an incident that was similar to this case?

Analytical questions (10 minutes)

1. Who are the primary individuals in this account? Secondary individuals?
2. How would you describe these characters?
3. Which individual do you identify with? What is it about him or her that you relate to?
4. What are the significant issues being raised in this account?

Integrative questions (20 minutes)

1. What dynamics may have contributed to the situation? What may be prompting Dr. Martin to use other's materials and pass them off as his own?
2. Is the McDonald's disillusionment with Dr. Martin legitimate and if so, to what extent?
3. What insights do the following passages offer? 2 Timothy 4:1–5; 1 Corinthians 1:26–2:5; Acts 4:32–5:11

Resolution questions (20 minutes)

1. What are the possibilities for resolving this situation?
2. What principles or guidelines should be considered so that preachers can take advantage of available resources while remaining authentic?
3. What are the possible effects of Dr. Martin's continued practice on his congregation? What results and/or consequences may occur if he persists in his current sermon preparation?

I value your thoughts about what you've just read.
Please email me at *zauthor@zondervan.com*.

NOTES

ACKNOWLEDGMENTS

1. Tobias Wolf, *Old School* (New York; Vintage Contenporaries, 2003), 144.

1 SCENES OF SERMON STEALING

1. There are questions at the end of each chapter and a case study in the Appendix to help you reflect on the issues raised in this book. The case includes teaching notes and questions.

2 THE LONG LEGACY OF SERMON STEALING

1. Many thanks to Tom Lehrer for permission to quote from this song. This portion is also quoted by Trudy Lieberman, "Plagiarize, Plagiarize, Plagiarize … Only Be Sure to Call It Research," *Columbia Journalism Review* 34, no. 2 (July August 1995): 21.
2. Mark Twain, *The Autobiography of Mark Twain* (New York: Washington Square Press, 1961), 164. I'm grateful to Jeffrey D. Arthurs for sharing with me this insight on Mark Twain.
3. Brett Martel, "Best-Selling Auth Stephen Ambrose Dies," *Salem News* (14 October 2002), A13.
4. Peter Schworm, "E. E. Cummings Scholar Accused of Plagiarism," *Boston Globe* (15 April 2005), B1.
5. David Mehegan, "After Duplicated Words, Words of Apology: Harvard Writer Says She 'Internalized' an Earlier Novel," *Boston Globe* (25 April 2006), A1, A6; idem, "Harvard Author's Apology Not Accepted: Publisher of Earlier Works Rejects View That Similarities Were Accidental," *Boston Globe* (26 April 2006), F1, F8; Motoko Rich and Dinitia Smith, "First, Idea, Plot and Characters. Then, a Book Needs an Author," *New York Times* (27 April 2006),

A1, A16; Dinitia Smith, "Copying Wasn't Intentional, A Harvard Novelist Says," *New York Times* (25 April 2006), National Report, A14; Dinitia Smith, "Novelist Says She Read Copied Book Several Times," *New York Times* (27 April 2006), A16; Lisa Wangsness, "In Many Ways, Parallels in 'Opal,' 'Sloppy Firsts' Are Striking: Two Novels Have a Teenage Heroine, Similar Encounters," *Boston Globe* (25 April 2006), A6–A7.

6. David Mehegan, "Harvard Novelist's Book Deal Canceled," *Boston Globe* (3 May 2006), A1, A18; idem, "Student Novelist's Book to Be Recalled," *Boston Globe* (28 April 2006), A1, A15.

7. Elizabeth Blair, "Suing for a Punchline: Leno, NBC Target Joke Books," *All Things Considered* (9 January 2007).

8. Sam Fulwood III, "Plagiarism Playing by the Rules," *Black Issues Book Review* 5, no. 5 (September October 2003): 24–25.

9. Kathy Slobogin, "Survey: Many Students Say Cheating's OK," *CNN.com* (5 April 2002), archives.cnn.com/2002/fyi/teachers.ednews/04/05/highschool.cheating/

10. Fulwood, "Plagiarism Playing by the Rules," 24–25.

11. Hunter Beckelhymer, "No Posturing in Borrowed Plumes," *The Christian Century* 41, no. 5 (6 February 1974): 138–42.

12. Seth Sutel, "Two Top Editors Resign at USA Today," *Boston Globe* (23 April 2004), A3. See the related story, Tony Carnes, "Jack Kelley's Tangled Web: Discredited USA Today Journalist Turns to Christian Colleagues for Support," *Christianity Today* 48(May 2004): 58–60.

13. Lieberman, "Plagiarize, Plagiarize, Plagiarize," 22.

14. Michael Levenson, "Worcester Newspaper Fires Reporter: Plagiarized Works, T & G Editor Says," *Boston Globe* (4 February 2005), B2. Another case of plagiarism is *Boston Globe* columnist Ron Borges, who plagiarized from Seattle Seahawks writer Mike Sando's article in the *News Tribune of Tacoma*. See also Michael Paulson, "Globe Suspends Sports Reporter Borges: Newspaper Editor Cites Plagiarism," *Boston Globe* (6 March 2007), B2.

15. Seth Mnookin, "The Times Bomb," *Newsweek* (26 May 2003), 41–51.

16. Jenna Russell, "BC Professor Recycled Ideas, Society Finds," *Boston Globe* (6 January 2005), B1.

17. Edward Rothstein, "Plagiarism That Doesn't Add Up," *New York Times* (9 March 2002), A17.

18. "Accreditation Update," *The Chronicle of Higher Education* (4 February 2005), A27. See also: Beth Kormanik, "Edward Waters Copied Report Crucial to Future," *The Florida Times-Union* (17 October 2004, modified 7 December 2004); idem, "Edward Waters Loses Its Accreditation," *The Florida Times-Union* (8 December 2004); idem, "Edward Waters Loses Its Accreditation," *The Florida Times-Union* (10 December 2004); idem, "Edward Waters President Resigns," *The Florida Times-Union* (8 February 2005).

19. "College Head Resigns over Attribution Flap," *Boston Globe* (2 October 2002), A2; "College President Admits Using Uncredited Sources in a Speech," *Boston Globe* (25 November 2002), A3.

20. Bryan Bender and Kevin Barton, "Soldier at Heart of Exam Inquiry Voices Defiance," *Boston Globe* (23 July 2007), A1, A6.

21. Bryan Bender and Kevin Barton, "Army Probes Alleged Exam Cheating," *Boston Sunday Globe* (22 July 2007), A1, A11. Chrysler faced disciplinary action and pulled the tests from the Internet site. See also: Bryan Bender, "Soldier in Cheating Probe Pulls Tests, Answers from Website," *Boston Globe* (27 July 2007), A5.

22. "The Charge of Plagiarism against Dr. Paley," *Methodist Quarterly Review* 31 (January 1849): 159. The argument is taken up in the journal *Athenaeum*.

23. Henry J. Fox, "Plagiarism and the Law of Quotation," *Methodist Quarterly Review* 61 (January 1879): 68.

24. Tom Coyne, "Plagiarism Question Prompts Notre Dame to Review Article: Theologian Says Group Targets Him," *Boston Globe* (24 January 2006), A5.

25. John W. Kennedy, "AMG Compensates Moody for Plagiarism," *Christianity Today* 39, no. 7 (19 June 1995): 42.

26. "Separate but Equal," *Update: A Quarterly Journal on New Religious Movements* 7, no. 2 (June 1983): 31.

27. Raymond Bailey, "Plagiarism," William H. Willimon and Richard Lischer, eds., *Concise Encyclopedia of Preaching* (Louisville, KY: Westminster John Knox, 1995), 374.

28. Fox, "Plagiarism and the Law of Quotation," 68.

29. I am grateful to Brian Stewart of Camden, Australia, for this ditty. Actually, Spurgeon considered people who purchased sermons and preached them as their own as problematic. See also: Charles Haddon Spurgeon, *Eccentric Preachers* (London: Passmore and Alabaster, 1897), 18–19.

30. John A. Broadus, *A Treatise on the Preparation and Delivery of Sermons* (New York: A. C. Armstrong & Son, 1889).

31. Brian Stewart, email message to the author, 28 July 2003. Stewart shares this account from his days in seminary.

32. Richard Lischer, "How the Preacher King Borrowed Sermons," *The Christian Ministry* 28, no. 1 (January–February 1997): 19–21. See also: Keith D. Miller, *Voice of Deliverance: The Language of Martin Luther King, Jr. and Its Sources* (New York: Free Press, 1992).

33. Dean Smith, "An Era When the Art of the Sermon Has Declined," *New York Times* (30 March 2002), A14.

34. "Clayton Pastor Resigns, Admits Plagiarizing Sermons," *Jefferson City News Tribune — Online Edition* (11 November 2001).

35. Danny Hakim, "Clergyman Is Accused of Plagiarism," *New York Times* (13 March 2002), A14. See also: Michael H. Hodges, "Troubles Split Cranbrook Church," *Detroit News* (25 March 2002); Alexa Capeloto, "Rector's Ethics Are Questioned: Bloomfield Parishioners Charge He Plagiarized; He Is Suspended," *Detroit Free Press* (1 March 2002).

36. "Disciples Moderator Sorry for Plagiarism," *The Christian Century* 120, no. 18 (6 September 2003): 15.

37. "Pastor Resigns after Admitting Plagiarism," *The Christian Century* 121, no. 112 (15 June 2004): 16. See also: Associated Press, "Minister Resigns Because of Plagiarism," *Portsmouth Herald* (15 May 2004), 1.

38. Jamie Dean, "Rev. Glenn Wagner Resigns from Calvary Church, Admits Plagiarism: Pastor of Charlotte Mega-Church Says Depression Led to Deceit," *The Charlotte World* (17 September 2004), 6.

39. Richard C. Dujardin, "Unitarian Minister Who Plagiarized May Be Forced Out," *The Providence Journal* (20 April 2007), A-01; idem, "Minister Resigns over Plagiarized Sermons," *The Providence Journal* (28 April 2007), A-04; idem, "Clergy Tap Variety of Sources for Sermons," *The Providence Journal* (6 May 2007), B-01.

40. Amy Joyce, "Lying on the Job Is a Fact but Dealing with It Is Tricky," *Boston Sunday Globe* (9 April 2006), G4; Associated Press, "New Reports of Medal Fraud Bring Calls for Tougher Laws," *New York Times* (1 May 2006), A16.

41. Kathy Slobogin, "Survey: Many Students Say Cheating's OK."

42. Richard A. Posner, *A Little Book of Plagiarism* (New York: Pantheon, 2007), 11.

43. Ibid., 15.

44. Ibid., 20.

45. Ibid., 37.

46. Ibid., 42.

47. Twain, *The Autobiography of Mark Twain*, 165.

48. Lieberman, "Plagiarize, Plagiarize, Plagiarize," 23.

49. Malcolm Gladwell, "Something Borrowed: Should a Charge of Plagiarism Ruin Your Life?" *The New Yorker* (22 November 2004), 48.

50. Levenson, "Worcester Newspaper Fires Reporter," B2.

51. Andrew Watterson Blackwood, *The Preparation of Sermons* (New York: Abingdon-Cokesbury, 1958). See William M. Ramsay, *St. Paul, the Traveller and the Roman Citizen* (New York: G. P. Putnam's Sons, 1901), 242.

52. Bailey, "Plagiarism," 375.

53. James W. Cox, *Preaching* (San Francisco: Harper & Row, 1985). See also: Augustine, *On Christian Doctrine* (New York: Liberal Arts Press, 1958), 166–68.

54. Lischer, "How the Preacher King Borrowed Sermons," 21.

55. Carter Shelley, "Preaching and Plagiarism: A Guide for Introduction to Preaching Students," *Homiletic* 27, no. 2 (Winter 2002): 4. See also: Andrew Fleming West, *Alcuin and the Rise of Christian Schools* (New York: Charles Scribner's Sons, 1899), 91.

56. E. C. Dargan, *A History of Preaching* (New York: A. C. Armstrong & Son, 1905), I:309; see also 187.

57. Lischer, "How the Preacher King Borrowed Sermons," 21. See also: Hughes Oliphant Old, *The Reading and Preaching of the Scriptures in the Worship of the Church*; Volume 4, *The Age of the Reformation* (Grand Rapids: Eerdmans, 2002), 12–16.

58. Shelley, "Preaching and Plagiarism," 4. Donne quote from: H. M. Paull, *Literary Ethics: A Study in the Growth of the Literary Conscience* (Port Washington, NY: Kennikat, 1968), 93.

59. Walter Wiest and Elwyn Smith, *Ethics in Ministry: A Guide for the Professional* (Minneapolis: Fortress, 1990), 40.

60. Joseph Gowan, *Homiletics or The Theory of Preaching* (London: Elliot Stock, 1922), 218–19.

61. Webb B. Garrison, "Plagiarism and the Development of Originality," *Religion in Life* 21, no. 4 (Autumn 1952): 574. See John Milton, *Areopagitica* (1644) (Oxford: Clarendon, 1917), 41.

62. Benjamin Franklin, "The Autobiography of Benjamin Frank-

lin." In *Harvard Classics the Five Foot Shelf of Books*, ed. Charles W. Eliot, vol. 1 (New York: P. F. Collier and Son, 1909), 98–99.

63. Gowan, *Homiletics or The Theory of Preaching*, 220.

64. Tom Younger, "Why I Use Other People's Stuff," *Leadership* 15, no. 1 (Winter 1994): 66.

65. William H. Willimon, "Borrowed Thoughts on Sermonic Borrowing," *The Christian Ministry* vol. 28, no. 1 (January–February 1997): 16.

66. Fulwood, "Plagiarism Playing by the Rules," 24–25.

67. Gerald L. Zelizer, "Sermon Sharing: Timesaver or Sin?" usatoday. com. Posted 26 March 2002 www.usatoday.com/news/comment /2002/03/27/ncguest1.htm

68. Cox, *Preaching*. See also: Willard A. Pleuthner, *Building Up Your Congregation* (Chicago: Wilcox & Follett, 1951), 117–18.

69. Hakim, "Clergyman Is Accused of Plagiarism," A14.

70. Anne Hiemstra Lynch, "Plagiarized Sermons No Small Matter," *Detroit Free Press* (15 March 2002).

71. David S. Blanchard, "Letter to the Editor: Secondhand Sermons," *New York Times* (19 March 2002), A26.

72. Gowan, *Homiletics or The Theory of Preaching*, 214–15.

73. Ibid., 216–17. See *The Clergyman's Instructor, or, a Collection of Tracts on the Ministerial Duties* (Oxford: Oxford Univ. Press, 1843), 247–49.

74. Donald Joseph McGinn, *The Admonition Controversy* (New Brunswick, NJ: Rutgers Univ. Press, 1949), 184.

75. Lischer, "How the Preacher King Borrowed Sermons," 21.

76. Ilion T. Jones, *Principles and Practice of Preaching* (Nashville: Abingdon, 1956), 145. See also: George E. Sweazey, *Preaching the Good News* (Englewood Cliff, NJ: Prentice-Hall, 1976), 188.

77. David Runk, "Rector's Suspension Raises Questions about Plagiarism," *Detroit Free Press* (15 March 2002).

78. Ibid.

79. Fox, "Plagiarism and the Law of Quotation," 67.

3 GIVE ME A DEFINITION, PLEASE!

1. Gowan, *Homiletics or The Theory of Preaching*, 206.

2. Ibid., 189.

3. J. M. Driver, "Royal Seizure; Or, The Ethics of Plagiarism," *Methodist Quarterly* 74 (May 1892): 406.

4. John W. Etter, *The Preacher and His Sermon* (Dayton: United Brethren Publishing House, 1891), 110.

5. Driver, "Royal Seizure; Or, The Ethics of Plagiarism," 415–16.

6. Garrison, "Plagiarism and the Development of Originality," 576. See also: *American Magazine* (February 1937), 168.

7. R. W. Dale, *Nine Lectures on Preaching* (London: Hodder and Stoughton, 1907), 297–98.

8. Thomas G. Long, "Stolen Goods: Tempted to Plagiarize," *The Christian Century* 124, no. 8 (17 April 2007): 20; See also: Barbara Bate, "Preaching: When Does Borrowing Become Stealing?" *Circuit Rider* 17, no. 8 (October 1993): 4–6.

9. Steve Sjogren, "Don't Be Original — Be Effective!" *Rick Warren's Ministry ToolBox*, http://www.pastors.com/RWMT/article.asp?ArtID=9230

10. Thanks to Calvin W. S. Choi for this information. Pastor Choi refers to a book written by Kyung Jae Yoo, et al., *The Sermons of the Sixteen Preachers of the Korean Church* (Seoul: The Christian Literature Society of Korea: Seoul, 2004). The book, written in Korean, evaluates the sixteen best preachers in Korea (thanks to Reverend Choi for translating the title). Regarding preaching and plagiarism in Korea, Pastor Choi states, "I remember an incident where a pastor used to copy other's sermon during his seminary years as he was church planting. He didn't have time to prepare his sermon but later on he realized it was unethical so he told his congregation. Fortunately, people appreciated his honesty and he is still serving there.... Preaching someone else's sermon is generally unacceptable in Korean culture but sadly preachers do it anyway knowingly and unknowingly." Calvin W. S. Choi, email message to author, 7 July 2007.

11. Jung Young Lee, *Korean Preaching: An Interpretation* (Nashville: Abingdon, 1997), 87.

12. Ibid., 87–88.

13. Kenton C. Anderson, "Squeaky Clean: Essential Areas of Focus for the Preacher Who Wants to Do Right," Haddon Robinson and Craig Brian Larson, eds., *The Art and Craft of Biblical Preaching: A Comprehensive Resource for Today's Communicators* (Grand Rapids: Zondervan, 2005), 87.

14. Twain, *The Autobiography of Mark Twain*, 164–65.

15. Ibid., 165.

16. Henry J. Fox, "Plagiarism and the Law of Quotation," *Methodist*

Quarterly Review 60 (October 1878): 653.

17. George E. Sweazey, *Preaching the Good News* (Englewood Cliff, NJ: Prentice-Hall, 1976), 187.

18. Peter Shaw, "Plagiary," *The American Scholar* 52, no. 2 (Summer 1982): 327.

19. Garrison, "Plagiarism and the Development of Originality," 575.

20. Lischer, "How the Preacher King Borrowed Sermons," 21.

21. Haddon Robinson, "Using Someone Else's Sermon: What is Plagiarism," Haddon Robinson and Craig Brian Larson, eds., *The Art and Craft of Biblical Preaching: A Comprehensive Resource for Today's Communicators* (Grand Rapids: Zondervan, 2005), 586.

22. Gillian Silverman, "It's a Bird, It's a Plane, It's Plagiarism Buster!" *Newsweek* (15 July 2002), 12.

23. Fulwood, "Plagiarism Playing by the Rules," 24.

24. Bailey, "Plagiarism," 374.

25. Woodrow Michael Kroll, *Prescription for Preaching* (Grand Rapids: Baker, 1980), 134.

26. Craig Brian Larson, "Plagiarism, Shmagiarism: The Why and When of Giving Credit," PreachingToday.com, www.preachingtoday.com/skills/specialtopics/200503.48.html#

27. Wiest and Smith, *Ethics in Ministry: A Guide for the Professional*, 41.

28. Associated Press, "Minister Resigns because of Plagiarism," *Portsmouth Herald* (15 May 2004).

29. Arthur S. Hoyt, *The Preacher: His Person, Message, and Method* (New York: MacMillan, 1909), 364.

30. Broadus, *A Treatise on the Preparation and Delivery of Sermons*, 138.

31. Younger, "Why I Use Other People's Stuff," 66–67.

32. Eugene L. Lowry, "Preaching or Reciting? Theft in the Pulpit," *The Christian Ministry* 22, no. 2 (March–April 1991): 9.

33. Bailey, "Plagiarism," 374.

34. Robinson, "Using Someone Else's Sermon," 586.

35. Lowry, "Preaching or Reciting?" 12.

36. Robinson, "Using Someone Else's Sermon," 586.

37. Anderson, "Squeaky Clean," 87.

38. Sweazey, *Preaching the Good News*, 187.

39. Cornelius Plantinga Jr., *Not the Way It's Supposed to Be: A Breviary of Sin* (Grand Rapids: Eerdmans, 1995), 13.

40. Ibid., 2.

41. Ibid., 27.

4 INTEGRITY IN PLAGIARISM AND PREACHING

1. Mark A. Taylor, "From the Editor: The Problems with Original Preaching," *Christian Standard* (2 October 2005), 627.

2. Mike Graves, "Preaching and Plagiarizing," *The Clergy Journal* (September 2004), 19. On this matter of the preacher's soul and the priorities of ministry, every pastor will benefit from reading Richard Baxter, *The Reformed Pastor*, first published in 1656.

3. Eugene H. Peterson, *Working the Angles: The Shape of Pastoral Integrity* (Grand Rapids: Eerdmans, 1987), 2.

4. David Hansen, *The Art of Pastoring: Ministry without all the Answers* (Downers Grove, IL: InterVarsity Press, 1994), 17.

5. Peterson, *Working the Angles*, 5.

6. Hansen, *The Art of Pastering*, 20.

7. Cary Dunlap, "When Pastors Plagiarize," *Rev.* (January–February 2005): 104.

8. Robinson, "Using Someone Else's Sermon," 586.

9. Jamie Buckingham, "Pulpit Plagiarism," *Leadership* 4 (Summer 1983): 66.

10. Robert Robinson, "Come, Thou Fount of Every Blessing," 1759, the third verse.

11. Dean, "Rev. Glenn Wagner Resigns from Calvary Church, Admits Plagiarism," 6.

12. Haddon W. Robinson, "Competing with the Communication Kings," *Making a Difference in Preaching*, ed. Scott M. Gibson (Grand Rapids: Baker, 1999), 109.

13. Thanks, Tom Haugen. I know this quote isn't original with you, but I know you've reminded me of the truth of it many times.

14. Kroll, *Prescription for Preaching*, 134.

15. Raymond Bailey, "Whatever Happened to Intellectual Honesty in the Sermon?" *Homiletic* 15 (Summer 1990): 2. See also: James T. Cleland, *Preaching to Be Understood* (Nashville and New York: Abingdon, 1965), 66–67.

16. Stephen L. Carter, *Integrity* (New York: Basic Books, 1996), 4.

17. 1 Corinthians 2:1–5.

18. Peterson, *Working the Angles*, 12.

19. Thanks, Stephen J. Sebastian.

20. Younger, "Why I Use Other People's Stuff," 66.

21. Cox, *Preaching*, 33.

SHOULD WE USE SOMEONE ELSE'S SERMON?

22. Laurie Tiberi, "Borrowing Is OK—Lying Is Not," *The Christian Ministry* 28, no. 1 (January–February 1997): 17–18.

23. Billy Graham, *Just As I Am: The Autobiography of Billy Graham* (New York: HarperSanFrancisco & Zondervan, 1997), 723.

24. Lori Carrell, *The Great American Sermon Survey* (Wheaton, IL: Mainstay Church Resources, 2000), 116. Carrell notes, "A third of responding preachers say their education was not adequate for sermon preparation and delivery."

25. Wayne Harvey, "Illustrating with Integrity and Sensitivity: Seven Questions for Staying above Reproach," Haddon Robinson and Craig Brian Larson, eds. *The Art and Craft of Biblical Preaching: A Comprehensive Resource for Today's Communicators* (Grand Rapids: Zondervan, 2005), 522.

26. Daniel P. Kidder, *A Treatise on Homiletics* (New York: Eaton & Mains, 1864), 388.

27. Darryl Dash, "Confessions of a Sermon Thief," *Preaching* 20, no. 2 (September–October 2004), 20.

28. A. J. Gordon, "Homiletic Habit," *The Watchword* 11, no. 6 (August 1887): 124.

29. Karl Barth, *Homiletics*, trans. Geoffrey W. Bromiley and Donald E. Daniels (Louisville, KY: Westminster John Knox, 1991), 83.

30. Driver, "Royal Seizure; Or, The Ethics of Plagiarism," 418.

31. Lila Arzua, "Preaching by Committee: More Pastors Use Group Approach, Multimedia Presentation," *The Washington Post* (5 December 2004), C–1, 11.

32. Thomas C. Oden, *Ministry through Word & Sacrament*, Classical Pastoral Care Series, vol. 2 (New York: Crossroad, 1989), [Luther, WA 53, p. 218; WLS 3, #3547, p. 1110], 39.

33. Brandon Cash, "Toward a Lifetime of Fruitful Preaching: Equipping Preachers to Engage Regularly the Biblical Languages," *The Journal of the Evangelical Homiletics Society* 7, no. 2 (September 2007): 29.

34. Blackwood, *The Preparation of Sermons*, 245.

35. Haddon W. Robinson, *Biblical Preaching: The Development and Delivery of Expository Messages*, 2nd ed. (Grand Rapids: Baker, 1980, 2001), 21.

36. Harry S. Stout, *The New England Soul: Preaching and Religious Culture in Colonial New England* (New York: Oxford, 1986), 35.

37. Garrison, "Plagiarism and the Development of Originality," 578.

38. Graves, "Preaching and Plagiarizing," 19.

39. Willimon, "Borrowed Thoughts on Sermonic Borrowing," 14–16.

40. Garrison, "Plagiarism and the Development of Originality," 577.

41. Robinson, "Using Someone Else's Sermon," 586.

42. Lowry, "Preaching or Reciting?" 10; See also: Graves, "Preaching and Plagiarizing," 18–19.

43. Graves, "Preaching and Plagiarizing," 19.

44. Broadus, *A Treatise on the Preparation and Delivery of Sermons*, 142.

45. Buckingham, "Pulpit Plagiarism," 61.

46. Thanks to Lee Eclov for helpful questions in this area of concern.

47. Mike Woodruff and Steve Moore, "Plagiarism, the Pulpit, and How to Appropriate Others' Ideas Appropriately," *Leadership* 24 (Winter 2003): 34.

48. Carter Shelley, "Preaching and Plagiarism," *Papers of the 36th Annual Meeting of the Academy of Homiletics in St. Louis, Missouri 29 November to 1 December 2001* (St. Louis: The Academy of Homiletics, 2001), 203. Shelley says, "Be careful not to name drop—if you met XXXX, don't describe him or her as 'a dear friend' unless you chat by telephone weekly."

49. Lowry, "Preaching or Reciting?" 12.

50. Ibid., 12.

51. Alexa Capeloto, "Rector's Ethics Are Questioned: Bloomfield Parishioners Charge He Plagiarized; He Is Suspended," *Detroit Free Press* (1 March 2002).

52. Runk, "Rector's Suspension Raises Questions about Plagiarism."

53. Ken Garfield, "Internet Inspiration for Preachers," *Charlotte Observer* (13 April 2002), F1.

54. Lugene Schemper, "Sermons on the Web," *Banner of Truth* (Winter 2003).

55. Blackwood, *The Preparation of Sermons*, 250.

56. Broadus, *A Treatise on the Preparation and Delivery of Sermons*, 142.

57. Smith, "An Era When the Art of the Sermon Has Declined," A14.

5 PREACHING IN A CUT-AND-PASTE WORLD

1. Sarah Horn, "Plagiarism in the Pulpit: The Epidemic Very Few Are Talking About," *Willow* 13, no. 3 (Summer 2006): 38.

2. Ibid., 38. The quote is from Jim Mellado, Willow Creek Association President.

3. Rick Ezell, "Constant Change: Where Preaching Has Been in

the Last 20 Years … and Where It's Going," *Preaching* 21, no. 1 (July August 2005): 26.

4. Dan Heneghan, letter. "Wonderful Sermon, Father … Where Did You Find It?" *Wall Street Journal* (24 November 2006), A13. Heneghan observes, "The Rev. Rick Warren's questioning of the merits of sermon attribution in his emailed view that preachers are 'not footnoting a term paper' suggests that his view of the truth is possibly more 'market-driven.'"

5. Suzanne Sataline, "That Sermon You Heard on Sunday May Be from the Web," *Wall Street Journal* (15 November 2006), A14. For example, Sataline observes, "Creativepastors.com, a nonprofit corporation owned by Fellowship Church, has posted revenue of $1.7 million since January 2004, and has 17,500 accounts, according to the church's pastor, Mr. Young."

6. Timothy F. Merrill, "The Pastor as Plagiarist," *Homiletics* 14, no. 4 (July August 2002): 73. Merrill is quoting from Stan Purdum, "As Found in *Homiletics*," *Homiletics* 11, no. 5 (September–October 1999): 7.

7. Joe E. Trull and James E. Carter, *Ministerial Ethics: Moral Formation for Church Leaders* (Grand Rapids: Baker, 2004), 100.

8. Long, "Stolen Goods: Tempted to Plagiarize," 18.

9. Richard Lischer, "What Shall I Borrow? Is It Tradition or Plagiarism?" *Circuit Rider* 17, no. 8 (October 1993): 8.

10. Tony Liston, "Confessions of an Addict: Why I Use Other Pastor's Sermons," *Rick Warren's Ministry Toolbox*, www.pastors.com/RWMT/article.asp?ArtID=9229

11. Even in the eighteenth century preachers were publishing others' sermons for profit—and it wasn't necessarily good stuff either. Reverend D. Rivers, a Dissenting minister in Britain, disdained the practice of preaching someone else's sermons. He attacked Dr. Trusler for printing "the most unspeakable trash that can be conceived." (*Memoirs of Living Authors* [1781]) quoted from: H. M. Paull, *Literary Ethics: Study in the Growth of the Literary Conscience* (London: Thornton Butterworth, 1928), 94.

12. Graves, "Preaching and Plagiarizing," 19.

13. Sataline, "That Sermon You Heard on Sunday May Be from the Web," A14. See also: Steve Sjogren, "Don't Be Original—Be Effective!" The websites include CreativePastors.com; Sermon Central.com; Pastors.com; and PreachingToday.com.

14. I doubt that Warren would consider his immensely popular book, *The Purpose-Driven Life*, as part of the public domain. If *The Purpose-Driven Life* were to be published by someone else — content and all with just a name change as author — that person would be slapped with a plagiarism suit. The question is, where would Warren draw the line? Warren has set a standard that is difficult to apply consistently. The problem with Warren is that the logic of application of "sharing" does not make sense. The deeper issue is ethics, not application.

15. This is a Haddon Robinsonism.

16. George R. Cannon Jr., "Preaching Someone Else's Sermons: The Problem with Plagiarism in the Pulpit," *Preaching* 22, no. 4 (January–February 2007): 38.

17. Sarah Horn, "Plagiarism in the Pulpit," 37.

18. "Disciples Moderator Sorry for Plagiarism," 15.

19. Lieberman, "Plagiarize, Plagiarize, Plagiarize," 24.

20. Dean, "Rev. Glenn Wagner Resigns from Calvary Church, Admits Plagiarism," 6. In this case, Wagner had been plagiarizing sermons for at least two years.

21. Plantinga, *Not the Way It's Supposed to Be*, 196–97.

22. Thanks, Tom Haugen.

23. Haddon Robinson is the source for this sage advice.

24. Keith Willhite, "Stop Preaching in the Dark (or: Gaining Feedback Isn't Enough)," *Preaching* 11, no. 6 (May–June 1996): 15–16. About 9 percent of those surveyed consult listeners as part of their sermon preparation, so says Lori Carrell in *The Great American Sermon Survey*, 110.

25. Lora-Ellen McKinney, *View from the Pew: What Preachers Can Learn from Church Members* (Valley Forge, PA: Judson, 2004), 11.

26. Andrew W. Blackwood, *Doctrinal Preaching for Today: Case Studies of Biblical Passages* (Nashville: Abingdon, 1956), 149. Originally in Bernard of Clairvaux, *Cantica Canticorum*, tr. Samuel J. Eales (London: Elliot Stock, 1895).

27. Long, "Stolen Goods: Tempted to Plagiarize," 20.

28. Barbara Mary Johnson, *Cheating: Maintaining Your Integrity in a Dishonest World* (Minneapolis: Augsburg, 1990), 53.

29. Ibid., 78.

30. Carter, *Integrity*, 22.

31. Keith I. Pohl, "When Borrowing Becomes Foolish," *Circuit Rider*

17, no. 8 (October 1993): 3.

32. Long, "Stolen Goods: Tempted to Plagiarize," 18.

33. Peterson, *Working the Angles*, 12.

34. For example, see Joe E. Trull and James E. Carter, *Ministerial Ethics: Moral Formation for Church Leaders* (Grand Rapids: Baker, 2004), 259–63. Trull and Carter provide examples of various denominational codes. See also: *Enrichment Journal* online: enrichmentjournal. ag.org/200404/200404_102_code_sb_sampl.cfm

35. Ibid., 221, 223–24.

36. Ibid., 229–39. Both the 1991 Disciples of Christ Code and the Code of Ethics for Ordained and Licensed Ministers and Lay Speakers in the Church of the Brethren have specific statements pledging that plagiarism is unacceptable. The 1991 American Baptist Churches in the U.S.A., the United Church of Christ Pastor's Code of Ethics, and the 1988 Unitarian Universalist Ministers' Code do not mention the matter of preaching and plagiarism.

37. Nolan B. Harmon, *Ministerial Ethics and Etiquette* (1928; Nashville: Abingdon, 1987), 145.

38. Carter, *Integrity*, 5.

AFTERWORD: KIDNAPPING WORDS

1. William Moats Miller, *Harry Emerson Fosdick: Preacher, Pastor, Prophet* (New York: Oxford, 1985), 337–38.

2. W. E. Sangster, *The Craft of the Sermon* (London: Epworth, 1954), 193–94.

3. "Dear Abby: Plagiarizing Priest Gives No Comfort to Mourning Daughter," *The Salem News* (25 January 2006), C4.

4. Sjogren, "Don't Be Original—Be Effective!"

5. The resources are plentiful. To cite a few, see Robert A. Harris, *Using Sources Effectively: Strengthening Your Writing and Avoiding Plagiarism*, 2nd edition (Glendale, CA: Pyrczak, 2005); *Questions and Answers on Copyright for the Campus Community* (Oberlin, OH: National Association of College Stores, 1994); acts.twu.ca/lbr.html is the site for Acts Seminaries, the Graduate School of Theological Studies of Trinity Western University in British Columbia. This site provides a helpful guide to writing and research; some of the computer programs adopted by colleges and universities include Turnitin and Copyscape; As for websites, see plagiarism.com. See also:

Julie Rawe, "A Question of Honor," *Time* (28 May 2007): 59–60; Taryn Plumb, "Schools Set Mouse Traps for Copycats," *Boston Sunday Globe* (30 April 2006), Globe North, 1, 13; "UNH Tests Plagiarism Detection Software," *Boston Globe* (21 February 2006), B2.

6. A 2005 survey conducted by the Center for Preaching at Gordon-Conwell Theological Seminary, 130 Essex Street, South Hamilton, MA.

7. Some churches are actually using video feed or projecting prerecorded videos of preachers preaching. This matter certainly raises questions about the nature of worship that are far beyond the scope of this book.

8. William Jones, letter. "Wonderful Sermon, Father ... Where Did You Find It?" *Wall Street Journal* (24 November 2006), A13.

Share Your Thoughts

With the Author: Your comments will be forwarded to the author when you send them to *zauthor@zondervan.com*.

With Zondervan: Submit your review of this book by writing to *zreview@zondervan.com*.

Free Online Resources at
www.zondervan.com

Zondervan AuthorTracker: Be notified whenever your favorite authors publish new books, go on tour, or post an update about what's happening in their lives at www.zondervan.com/authortracker.

Daily Bible Verses and Devotions: Enrich your life with daily Bible verses or devotions that help you start every morning focused on God. Visit www.zondervan.com/newsletters.

Free Email Publications: Sign up for newsletters on Christian living, academic resources, church ministry, fiction, children's resources, and more. Visit www.zondervan.com/newsletters.

Zondervan Bible Search: Find and compare Bible passages in a variety of translations at www.zondervanbiblesearch.com.

Other Benefits: Register to receive online benefits like coupons and special offers, or to participate in research.

ZONDERVAN®

ZONDERVAN.com/
AUTHORTRACKER
follow your favorite authors

CPSIA information can be obtained at www.ICGtesting.com
Printed in the USA
LVOW07s2028070314

376464LV00013B/249/P